连老外都在用的

社交信函大全

张成月　编著

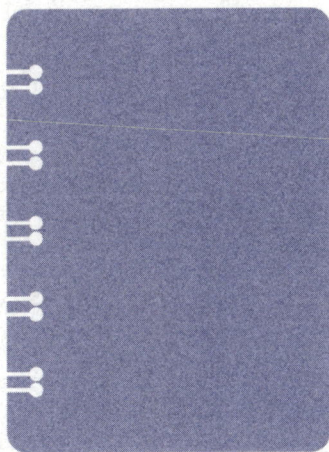

中国纺织出版社有限公司

图书在版编目（CIP）数据

连老外都在用的社交信函大全：汉、英 / 张成月编
著. --北京：中国纺织出版社有限公司，2022.6
ISBN 978-7-5180-6701-5

Ⅰ.①连… Ⅱ.①张… Ⅲ.①英语—书信—写作
Ⅳ.①H315

中国版本图书馆CIP数据核字（2019）第206740号

责任编辑：武洋洋　　责任校对：高　涵　　责任印制：储志伟

中国纺织出版社有限公司出版发行
地址：北京市朝阳区百子湾东里A407号楼　邮政编码：100124
销售电话：010—67004422　传真：010—87155801
http://www.c-textilep.com
中国纺织出版社天猫旗舰店
官方微博http://weibo.com/2119887771
三河市延风印装有限公司印刷　各地新华书店经销
2022年6月第1版第1次印刷
开本：710×1000　1/16　印张：15
字数：200千字　定价：45.00元

凡购本书，如有缺页、倒页、脱页，由本社图书营销中心调换

Preface
前 言

　　提到写英文书信，相信很多人都会有"这还不简单！"的观念，认为只要掌握了一定量的英语词汇，写封信还算什么难事？然而，到了真正下笔的时候，却发现无从下手。其实，就像学习英语本身一样，只要抓到诀窍和重点，写出完整又漂亮的英文书信绝对不是件难事！

　　这本《连老外都在用的社交信函大全》并非一本普通的英语书，它是一本绝对实用、绝对完整，连美国人都在看、都在用的书信大全集！编者首先将不同类型的书信格式详细地介绍给读者，让大家不再因为各种复杂的书信格式而感到迷茫。此外，虽然现在大多数公司都以电子邮件及部分纸本书信为主，但是传真的基本格式也是不可或缺的重点知识，在这本书中也做了详细的介绍。在"范本篇"中，编者列出了许多商业书信及其他书信类型的范例，以前可能你只会写申请信、感谢信，但是，现在你完全有能力写一封漂亮的求职信、产品推销信甚至是请柬。"缩写篇"中列出"商务英语缩写""考试缩写""职务用语缩写"等，方便读者随时查阅，找出自己最想表述的那个专业词汇，从而更好地辅助你写出专业的英文书信。

　　好了，既然连美国人都在用，那么就一起来体验这本书吧！

编著者

2022年5月

Contents
目 录

I

Chapter 2　范本篇

Chapter 3　缩写篇

Chapter 1

类别篇

Unit 1 纸本书信

Lesson 1 英文书信结构

📄 信头 Heading

信头是指写信人的地址和写信日期。一般写在信纸的右上方，先写地址后写日期，日期写在地址的下一行。地址应从小写到大，先写姓名、单位名称、门牌号码，再写街道、城镇、省或州及邮政编码，最后是国家名称。需要注意的是英国的时间写法是日、月、年的顺序，美国的写法是月、日、年。例如：

Mary King

No. 69 Wangcheng Street

Yangzhou

Jiangsu Province

225002

P. R. China

7th July, 2011/ July 7th, 2011

📍 信内地址 Inside Address

一般的社交信中，信内收信人的地址通常省略，但在公务信函中不可省略。信内地址要写出收信人的姓名和地址，并写在信头日期下方的左上角，与信头的书写要求一样，日期可以省略。

ⓐ 对方是公司个人的话，收信人要有名字、职位、公司名称、公司所在的街名、区名和市名。例如：

Miss Nancy A. Christian

Sales Manager

P&G

Overstone Court

Cardiff, Wales

UK

ⓑ 对方是公司无名的职员，但不知其姓名时，不需要收信人的名字，只需要写职位名称、公司名字、街道名、区名和市名。例如：

Advertising Manager

P&G

Overstone Court

Cardiff, Wales

UK

ⓒ 对方是公司时，只需要公司名，街道名，区名和市名。例如：

P&G

Overstone Court

Cardiff, Wales

UK

称谓 Salutation

称谓是对收信人的称呼。在信内地址下一两行处顶格写起，末尾用逗号或者冒号。

ⓐ 给公司写信：Dear Sirs,

ⓑ 给不知道名字的男性写信：Dear Sir,

ⓒ 给不知道名字的女性写信：Dear Madam,

ⓓ 给知道名字的男性写信：Dear Mr. Smith,

ⓔ 给知道名字的女性写信：Dear Miss Black（未婚），Dear Mrs. Black（已婚），

ⓕ 给朋友或者熟悉的人写信：Dear Smith,

正文 The Body

正文是书信的主体，用来表达写信人的思想，一般写在称谓的下一行。正文一般根据写信者所要表达的中心思想分段，使正文层次清晰，观点明确。正文开头要有一两句寒暄，然后开始写正题，结尾要有祝福和敬语。例如：

I am glad to get your new address. It's wonderful that you have a house of your own eventually. You must be very happy for living a new life in such nice surroundings. My wife and I are going to visit you and your new house soon.

I'm sending you a tea table for your living room. Please accept it as a token of my hearty congratulations on your residence changing.

My wife and I wish you everything goes well!

很高兴得知你家的新地址。你终于有了自己的房子，真是太棒了。现在你在如此舒适的环境中开始新生活，一定很开心吧！我和我太太近期登门拜访，顺便参观你的新居。

我寄给你一张茶几用来装饰客厅，作为你乔迁之喜的贺礼，敬请笑纳。

我和我太太祝你一切顺利！

💬 实用例句 The Opening Sentences & The Closing Sentences

常用开头语（The Opening Sentences）：

1. I have received your letter on 3rd August.

我已于8月3号收到你的来信。

2. I am very glad to receive your letter.

很高兴收到你的来信。

3. Many thanks for your last kind letter.

非常感谢你上一封来信。

4. Your letter came to me this morning.

今早收到你的来信。

5. I have been missing you a lot since we met last time.

自从上次见面后我一直在想你。

6. Sorry for delaying this letter so long.

这么晚才给你回信，深感歉意。

7. As I mentioned earlier about...

如我先前提及的关于……

8. We would like to inform you that...

我们想要通知你……

9. From your letter I learned that...

你的信中提到……

10. With great delight I learned that...

我得知……非常高兴。

常用结束语（The Closing Sentences）：

1. I am looking forward to hearing from you.

盼早日回信。

2. Hope to get your reply as soon as possible.

希望能尽快收到你的回复。

3. Hoping to hear from you soon.

希望尽早得到你的消息。

4. We look forward to your reply at your earliest convenience.

我们期待您及早回复。

5. Your early reply will be highly appreciated.

早日答复将不胜感激。

6. I look forward to our next meeting.

我非常期待我们的下次见面。

7. I hope everything will be well with you.

望您一切安好。

8. I wish you every success in the coming year.

祝您明年一切顺利。

9. Please remember me to your family.

请帮我问候您的家人。

10. Awaiting your good news.

等待您的好消息。

✉ 信尾客套语 Complimentary Close

信尾客套语写在信的左下角或右下角，表示写信人对收信人的一种礼貌客气或是亲昵的称呼。一般写于正文下面一、二行处，首字母大写，句尾用逗号。例如：

ⓐ 知道收信人的姓名时：Yours sincerely,

ⓑ 不知道收信人的姓名时：Yours faithfully,

ⓒ 收信人是关系比较亲密的好朋友或同事时：Best regards,

ⓓ 收信人是一个部门或整体时：Yours faithfully,

📝 签名 Signature

写信人在结束语正下方下面一至二行处，亲笔签上自己的姓名。公务信函中，签名下面还要有机打的姓名，以便识别；职务、职称等可打在姓名的下面。若是写信给亲朋好友，就不用机打了。

附言及附件 Postscript & Enclosure

ⓐ 随信如有附件，通常用"Encl."或"Enc."左顶格标注在签名下方一至二行处。两件或两件以上须标明数目。例如：Enc.: invoices 5（随信附带五张发票），Encl.: certificate（随信附带证书）。

ⓑ 信写完了，突然想起遗漏的事情，这时通常在信末签名下面几行，与正文齐头写上"P.S."，再写上遗漏的话。正式信函中，应尽量避免使用附言。

英文信件结构总图表

◆ 信头（Heading）

◆ 信内地址（Inside Address）

◆ 称谓（Salutation）

◆ 正文（The Body）

◆ 信尾客套语（Complimentary Close）

◆ 签名（Signature）

◆ 附件（Enclosure）

◆ 附言（Postscript）

读书笔记

Lesson 2　英文书信格式

英文书信格式与汉语书信格式不尽相同，或者说完全不同，大致可以分为以下三种：

齐头式 Block Form

信头、信内地址、称谓、正文（包括每段起始句）、结尾客套语、签名等各部分的左边均需上下对齐。这种形式便于打字，因此多用于商务书信。美国人及加拿大人多采用此种格式。例如：

Eric Northman

No.73 Yuyuan Road

Shanghai 200040

P. R. China

June 30th, 2011

Prof. David Harvey

307 Nottingham Avenue

North Hill Beach, Florida 33404

U.S.A.

Dear Professor Harvey,

　　Your speech this morning was exactly what we needed to hear about Global Environmental Protection. Each slide was clear and concise, and every point indicated current environmental problems. Furthermore, your handouts of the final conclusion would help us strengthen protection on our surrounding environment. I really appreciate your speech!

Yours sincerely,

Eric Northman

缩进式 Indented Form

信头和信内地址均较上一行缩进一些，一般缩进2~3个英文字母。正文每段开始行，一般缩进5个英文字母。例如：

> Eric Northman
> No.73 Yuyuan Road
> Shanghai 200040
> P. R. China
> June 30, 2011
>
> Prof. David Harvey
>   307 Nottingham Avenue
>   North Hill Beach, Florida 33404
>   U.S.A.
>
> Dear Professor Harvey,
>
>   Your speech this morning was exactly what we needed to hear about Global Environmental Protection. Each slide was clear and concise, and every point indicated current environmental problems. Furthermore, your handouts of the final conclusion would help us strengthen protection on our surrounding environment.
>
>   I really appreciate your speech!
>
> Yours sincerely,
> Eric Northman

读书笔记

折中式 Modified Form

它是上述两种形式的混合应用。这种形式的信头、信内地址、日期以及结束敬语的书写位置大致与缩进式相同，只是不采用字母缩进的方式。例如：

Eric Northman

No.73 Yuyuan Road

Shanghai 200040

P. R. China

June 30, 2011

Prof. David Harvey

307 Nottingham Avenue

North Hill Beach, Florida 33404

U.S.A.

Dear Professor Harvey,

    Your speech this morning was exactly what we needed to hear about Global Environmental Protection. Each slide was clear and concise, and every point indicated current environmental problems. Furthermore, your handouts of the final conclusion would help us strengthen protection on our surrounding environment.

    I really appreciate your speech!

Yours sincerely,

Eric Northman

读书笔记

Lesson 3 英文书信写作

英文书信写作基本原则

英文书信写作有五项基本原则，简称"5C原则"。

体贴（Consideration）：体贴是指写信者应设身处地为对方着想，尊重对方的风俗习惯，还应该考虑到收信者的文化程度、性别等因素。

简明（Conciseness）：简明是指写信者应用尽可能少的文字表达其必须传递的信息，避免书信过于冗长，还应该用简单常见的短单词代替复杂生僻的浮华表达，尽量避免意义重复的修饰词，做到行文流畅、言简意赅。

清晰（Clarity）：清晰是指写信者应将所需传递的信息表达清楚，以免对方产生误解。

礼貌（Courtesy）：礼貌是指写信者应避免使用伤害对方感情的表达，措辞上多选用礼貌委婉的词语，做到不卑不亢，落落大方。

正确（Correctness）：正确是指写信者要避免语法、拼写、标点符号错误，并且书信中引用的史料、数据等也应做到准确无误。

英文信封写法与格式

与中文信封相反，英文信封上寄信人的地址和姓名写在信封的左上角，收信人的地址和姓名写在信封的中间。地址应从小写到大，先写姓名、单位名称、门牌号码，再写街道、城镇、省或州及邮政编码，最后是国家名称。可在收信人姓名前加"To"，寄信人姓名前加上"From"。

From 寄信人地址（Sender's Name & Address）邮票（Stamp）

To 收信人地址（Recipient's Name & Address）

⚠ 英文信封写作注意事项

ⓐ 信封的地址多采用齐头式写法。

ⓑ 若想说明信件的类别、投递方式或其他有关情况，可在信封的左上角，即寄信人的姓名和地址下面注明。常见说明语有：Ordinary Mail（平信），Registered（挂号信），Immediate（急件），Express（特快专递），By Air Mail（航空信），Confidential（机密），Printed Matter（印刷品），Photos Enclosed, Please Do Not Bend（内附照片，请勿折叠），With Parcel（另附包裹），Private（私人信，亲启），Personal（私函）等。例如：

From Helen White

323 Zhongyang Road   Stamp

Gulou District, Nanjing 210009

P.R China

By Air Mail

                                                To Mr. Robert Hilton

                                                   405 Liberty Lane

                                                Wilmington, NC 28409

                                                        U.S.A

ⓒ 如果新建信件寄给第三者，再由第三者转交给收信人，则在收信人姓名下一行下先写上C/O（care of的缩写，表示"由……转交"），再写上转交人的姓名，此时的地址应写转交人的地址。例如：

From Helen White

323 Zhongyang Road   Stamp

Gulou District, Nanjing 210009

P.R China

Private

                                                To Mr. Robert Hilton

                                                   C/O John Wood

                                             302 Red, White and Blue Ave.

                                                Wilmington, NC 28409

                                                        U.S.A

---

d 如果信件不是通过邮寄，而是直接托某人转交，则信封上可以只写收信人的姓名，省略收信人的地址，然后在收信人姓名下一行先写上Kindness of, Politeness of, By Courtesy of 等表示"请……转交"意思的短语，再写上转交人的姓名。也可以在收信人姓名的上一行写上Please Forward（请转交……），此时可省略转交人姓名不写。例如：

Mr. Robert Hilton

Kindness of Mr. John Wood

或

Please Forward

Mr. Robert Hilton

✉ 英文书信折叠法

折叠信件装入信封时，不要折叠得过大或过小，也不要给收信人打开信封造成麻烦。最常用、最简单的折叠法是折叠两次，将信纸折成三等份。折叠时，将信纸正面向上，由信纸底端向上折叠至三分之一处，然后折叠信纸上端，将信纸折叠成"Z字形"三等份。

将折叠好的信件放入信封时要注意，信纸上端，即写有收信人姓名的一端要朝向信封开口，这样便于收信人拆信和读信。

读书笔记

Unit 2　电子邮件

Lesson 4　电子邮件的格式

发件时的电子邮件格式

To（收件人）：输入收件人的电子邮箱地址。

Cc（抄送）：输入接收抄送文件的人的电子邮箱地址，收件人知道此抄送信息。

Bcc（密送）：输入接收抄送文件的人的电子邮箱地址，收件人不知道此抄送信息。

Subject（主题）：输入邮件的简短概括介绍。

Message text area（正文）：输入邮件正文内容。

Attachments（附件）：上传邮件附带的附件文件。

收件时的电子邮件格式

From（发件人）：显示发件人的电子邮箱地址。

To（收件人）：显示收件人的电子邮箱地址。

Cc（抄送）：显示接收抄送文件的人的电子邮箱地址。

Date（时间）：显示邮件发送时的时间。

Subject（主题）：显示邮件的简短概括介绍。

Message text area（正文）：显示邮件正文内容。

Attachments（附件）：下载邮件附带的附件文件。

读书笔记

Lesson 5　电子邮件的注意事项

（1）邮件一定要有明确的主题，内容要言简意赅，真实反映邮件的内容等。千万不要不写主题，或是主题冗长、含义不清。

（2）信件结构要完整，称谓和署名不可少，收件人称呼要恰当。开头结尾要有问候语，这样能使邮件读起来更友好。电子邮件中对收信人的称谓，以及开头结尾的问候语与纸本书信的写作原则相同。

（3）根据收件人与自己的熟悉程度、等级关系、邮件的性质等因素，选择恰当的语气进行论述，要时刻站在收件人的立场上考虑。

（4）正文内容要简明扼要，行文通顺，最好能在一封邮件中将全部相关信息表达清楚、准确。若事情复杂，可分段列表进行说明，并保持段落的简洁。也可采用"倒金字塔式"的写作方式，先写重要内容，随着叙述的展开，重要性逐渐减弱。这种方式可以在有限的版面内尽快将信息传达给收件人。

（5）如果邮件带有附件，应在正文里提示收件人查看附件，并简要介绍附件内容。附件若是特殊格式文件，也要在正文中说明打开方式。附件文件的命名要让收件人一目了然，附件数目较多时应压缩打包再发送。

（6）收到他人邮件后应及时回复，理想的回复时间是两小时内；若事情复杂，不能确切回复，至少也应该及时回复收到，说明正在处理中。

范本一 | 分享好消息

Dear Diana,

I am very excited to tell you that I have been elected as the exchange student to America for one year. I feel so happy that I can study abroad and make new friends there. I can not help expecting my new life in America now.

Diana, you are my best friend and I will miss you there. The moment I settle down there, I will call you. Thank you so much for being my friend and let's keep in touch even though I am abroad. I will bring souvenir for you when I come back one year later.

Best regards,

Katherine

亲爱的戴安娜：

我非常激动地告诉你一个好消息，我们学校推选我为交换生去美国留学一年。我真的非常高兴能去国外学习并且在那认识新朋友，现在我已经不由自主地开始期待我的美国生活了。

戴安娜，你是我最好的朋友，我会想念你的，等我在那边安顿下来就给你打电话。谢谢你做我的朋友，即使我在国外我们也要保持联系，一年后回来时我会给你带礼物的。

祝你安好！

凯瑟琳

范本二 | 祝福他人

Dear Bill,

I take great pleasure in sending congratulations on your winning the scholarship to Harvard University.

I'm not surprised at all, and I'm all happy to get the good news. I know you have got excellent records for all the courses you took through your own industriousness and perseverance. It is really a great achievement for you. You richly deserve the award. I'm really proud of you.

Warmest congratulations.

Yours sincerely,

Charley

亲爱的比尔：

得知你获得哈佛大学的奖学金，我怀着十分喜悦的心情向你表示祝贺。

听到这个消息我一点也不惊讶，我由衷地为你感到高兴。我知道你通过自己的勤奋和毅力各门课程成绩都很优异，这真是一个巨大的成就。这绝对是你应得的荣耀，我真为你骄傲。

致以最热烈的祝贺！

谨启

查理

范本三 | 想念你

Dear Bella,

I've been missing you very much since you transferred to another school. We haven't contacted each other for a long time. How is everything going? I cherished the time when we were together and often thought back to the happy days of us. Now I'm writing to tell you that I really miss you. I have a lot to tell you and I can't help wondering if you feel the same way. No matter what your answer is or how you feel about me, just write to me. Awaiting for your mail.

Yours sincerely,

Tony

亲爱的贝拉：

自从你转学后，我十分想念你。我们好长时间没有联系了，你最近还好吗？我很珍惜过去我们在一起的时光，也经常回想起我们在一起快乐的日子。现在，我写这封信是因为我真的很想你。我有许多话想告诉你，也很想知道你是不是也有很多话对我讲。不管你的答案是什么，不论你对我的感觉如何，请写信给我。等待你的回信。

谨上！

托尼

范本四 | 感谢馈赠

Dear Jimmy,

Thank you very much for your present! I love the wooden Japanese kokeshi doll you brought me from Japan. It is cute and exquisite! The doll now on my bookcase is so attractive that it has won the compliments of every visitor to my home. Every time I look at the doll, I can't help thinking of you. You are always concerned about me even on a trip. I am so lucky to have you to be my best friend!

Thank you!

Best wishes,

Jena

亲爱的吉米：

非常感谢你的礼物！我非常喜欢你从日本带给我的木质日本木偶娃娃。它很可爱，也很精致！我把这个娃娃放置在我的书柜上，它非常吸引眼球，每个到我家做客的人都对它赞不绝口。每次我看见它，都会忍不住想起你。你人在旅途却还惦记着我，有你这样一个好友我感到非常幸运！

谢谢你！

诚挚的祝福

珍娜

范本五 | 佳节问候

Dear Jack,

Merry Christmas and happy New Year! Thank you for your patronage over the years. You've made my life more wonderful and harmonious with your kindheartedness and passion. We have developed good friendship and I look forward to enjoying it for years to come.

Best wishes for the New Year! May you and all your family members have a pleasant holiday.

Wish you happiness and prosperity in the coming year.

Best regards,

Ken

亲爱的杰克：

圣诞快乐！新年快乐！感谢你这些年给我的支持。你用你的善良和热情让我的生活变得更加精彩和谐。我们建立了深厚的友谊，我也盼望能在将来的日子里享受这份友谊。

新年之际送上我最诚挚的祝福！祝福你和家人节日愉快。

愿你在新的一年里事业兴旺，幸福美满！

献上最真挚的祝福

肯

读书笔记

Unit 3　传真

Lesson 6　传真的格式

To（收件人）：输入收件人的姓名。　　Fax（传真）：输入传真号码
From（发件人）：输入发件人的姓名。　Date（日期）：输入发件的日期
Subject（主题）：输入传真简短的概括介绍。Page（页数）：输入传真的页数
Cc（抄送）：输入接收抄送文件的人的姓名。
Message text area（正文）：输入传真正文内容。

读书笔记

Lesson 7　传真的注意事项

（1）传真发送前后均需要打电话确认。如果接收的人不在，在电话里要向对方说明。通话时态度一定要谦虚诚恳，切忌无精打采或用满不在乎的口气委托对方传达。

（2）注意认真确认对方的传真号码，不要发错。传真的开头要写明传真的单位或个人，包括地址、电话、电子邮箱等内容，便于给接收者明确的信息。

（3）传送多张资料时，为了保证传真接收者能够完整地接收信息，没有遗漏，必须写清楚传真的页数，便于接收者核对。同时要注意文字墨迹不要太淡，文字大小要适中，便于对方阅读。

（4）传真要主题明确，简洁地告知对方需要沟通的事件。内容要简洁明了，同时要包括需要表达的完整信息。内容的最后要写明传真的主要目的并附上问候语，表示对接收方的尊重。工作用的传真任何人都可能看到，所以不适合传送一些涉及个人隐私和机密的信息。感谢信、慰问信、吊唁信等一般不使用传真收或发。类似于寒暄、问候等礼节性的内容也不适合使用传真。

（5）接收传真后要在专门的《传真登记簿》上编号登记，做到页数完整、内容不遗漏。接收传真后要回电对方，一方面让对方放心，另一方面应择其重点复述一遍，尤其时间、地点、联系方式等要核对准确。

（6）收发传真时不要打手机、聊天等，不要在传真件上随意写画，保证传真件的整洁，做到及时有序。另外，要注意传真件的备份保存，确保清晰完整。

范本一 | 咨询产品使用情况

Dear Mr. Cooper,

　　We are honored that you have agreed to use our products. In order to know the demand of the customers better, and then improve the functions of our products, we hope that you can tell us something about the products, so we can do some research and improvement. Thank you!

Yours sincerely,

Mary

尊敬的库伯先生：

　　很高兴贵公司能够使用我们的产品。为了能够更好地了解顾客的需求，我们对产品功能进行了改进，希望您能够告知我们使用本公司产品的情况，以便我们进行调研和改进。谢谢！

敬上

玛丽

范本二 | 预订酒店住房

Dear Miss Lucy,

This is Flying Dream travel agency. We'd like to reserve ten double rooms (breakfast included). We will check in on May 1st and check out on May 4th. All charges are to be paid on my credit card. Please inform us if you don't have enough rooms for us. Thank you!

Best wishes,

Karoline

亲爱的露西小姐：

您好！我们是飞梦旅行社，我们想预约十间双人间（含早餐）。我们会在5月1日入住，5月4日离开，所有费用请用我的信用卡支付。如果房间不够请通知我们。谢谢。

祝好！

凯若琳

范本三 | 请人帮忙订购机票

Dear Vivian,

I will go to Beijing to attend a meeting next Monday. I would be obliged if you could book an economical class seat for me on a flight leaving Shanghai to Beijing on June 20. Please book the earliest flight if possible. Bank of China has been instructed to pay the fare and you can submit your account directly to them. Thank you very much!

Best wishes,

Nancy

亲爱的薇薇安：

下周一我要前往北京开会。如果你能帮我订一张6月20号由上海飞往北京的经济舱飞机票，我将不胜感激。如果可以的话，请帮我订最早的航班。我已经委托中国银行支付机票费，你可以把账单直接交给他们。非常感谢。

祝好！

南希

范本四 | 介绍新产品

Dear Mr. Andy,

I am so glad to inform you that recently we have got a batch of new fancy lamps. Compared with the previous lamps, these are more beautiful and functional. Not only the appearance is more delicate, but the light is much softer. We have enclosed our catalogue which introduces the lamp more specifically. Please inform us if you're interested in our new products and we will send you some samples. Looking forward to your reply.

Best wishes,

Alice

尊敬的安迪先生：

很高兴通知您，我公司新进了一批装饰灯。相较以前的那些，这些灯具更加美观和实用。它们不仅外观更精致，灯光也更柔和。我们也传真了这种灯更详细的介绍。如果您感兴趣，请告诉我们，我们会给您寄一些样品。期待您的回复。

祝好！

爱丽丝

范本五 | 寻求合作

Dear Miss Shirley,

Recently our company has launched a project to develop a new kind of software and we need a cooperative partner to accomplish this project. I think your company is our best choice, because you do well in software developing. Here we sincerely invite you to be our partner. We have enclosed our catalogue, which introduces our company and this project in detail. I will appreciate it if you agree to this cooperation. I'm looking forward to your reply.

Yours sincerely,

Tom

尊敬的雪莉小姐：

　　最近我公司启动了一个开发新软件的项目，需要一个合作伙伴来共同完成这个项目。因为贵公司在软件开发方面非常出色，我想贵公司是我们最好的选择，在此真诚邀请贵公司合作。我们也传真了关于我公司和这个项目更详细的介绍，若贵公司能同意这次合作，我们将不胜感激。期待您的回复。

谨上！

汤姆

读书笔记

Chapter 2

范本篇

Unit 4　社会公关书信

Lesson 8　介绍信

如何写介绍信

ⓐ首先写明这封介绍信的目的，说明写信人与被介绍者的关系。

ⓑ写明被介绍人在各个方面的情况，帮助对方对其有个大致的印象。

ⓒ希望收信方能够给予被介绍者帮助及支持，对此表示感谢。

实用例句

1. The purpose of this letter is to introduce my friend Lucy. She will be a member of your company, and I hope you can offer her some help.

   我写这封信的目的是想要向你介绍我的朋友露西。她将成为你们公司的一员，我希望你能多帮帮她。

2. She is active, enthusiastic and honest. But sometimes she may make some little mistakes. Therefore, I want you to help and teach her when necessary.

   她积极主动、富有激情，而且又诚实。但是有时候会犯点小错，所以我希望必要时你能帮助她，教教她。

3. You will be impressed by the charming girl who is beautiful, honest and hard-working. But she still has a lot of things to learn. I think you can be a good teacher. Thank you very much.

   你将会对这个漂亮、诚实、努力的女孩印象深刻的。但是她还有很多地方需要学习。我想你会是她的好老师。非常感谢。

4. We have worked together for five years and I know him quite well. He is a good business partner, so I want to introduce him to you.

   我们在一起工作已经五年了，彼此都非常熟悉。他是个很好的生意伙伴，所以我想把他介绍给你。

5. He is an excellent person who is very good at communicating with people. And he was also the best salesman in his company. I think he will be helpful to you.

他是个很不错的人，非常善于与人交流，曾经是他们公司销售业绩最好的一个。我想他可能能帮助你。

6. He is one of my students who is very smart and skilled at communication. I hope you can offer a position in your company for him.

他是我的一个学生，非常聪明，善于交流。我希望你能在你们公司帮他找个职位。

7. Thank you very much. And I suggest we should have a dinner so I can formally introduce her to you. Please call me if it is convenient for you.

非常感谢。我提议我们一起吃个晚饭，这样我就可以把她正式介绍给你。如果哪天方便的话，请打给我。

8. I think he is the person that you are looking for, so I want to give you some information about him. Maybe you will be interested in him.

我认为他正是你要找的人，所以我想给你一些有关他的信息，也许你会对他感兴趣。

9. Although he has just joined the company for few months, he is a quick-learner. His performance is also very good. In his daily life, he also gets along with the colleagues very well. So I want to introduce him into your company.

他虽然刚进公司不久，但是他学习能力非常强，工作也非常出色，生活中与同事们相处得非常好。所以我想把他介绍到你们公司任职。

10. I can guarantee that he is a very diligent and hardworking person who will make good performances in your company. I hope you can consider this.

我可以保证他是个非常勤快和努力的人，一定会给你们公司带来业绩。希望你能考虑一下。

范本一 | 介绍朋友请求关照

Dear Lily,

   I want to introduce my friend Lucy to you. She is my best friend who is beautiful, honest and hard-working. Next week she will be a member of your company. I hope you can help me to take care of her. If she has any problem, I hope you can give her a hand. She is very smart and will learn everything quickly if she has a good teacher. And I think you can be a good teacher for her.

Thank you very much. And I suggest we should have a dinner so I can formally introduce her to you. Please call me if it is convenient for you.

Best wishes,
Abby

亲爱的莉莉：

我想要向你介绍一下我的朋友露西。她是我最好的朋友，漂亮、诚实又勤奋，下周她将会去你们公司上班，我希望你能帮我关照一下她。如果她有什么问题的话，请帮她一把。她很聪明，要是有人教她的话，她学东西很快。我想你会是一位好老师。

非常感谢。我建议我们一起吃个晚饭，这样我就可以把她正式介绍给你。如果哪天方便的话，请打给我。

祝好！
艾比

Dear Abby,

I am happy to hear from you. I'm glad you will introduce your best friend to me. I am looking forward to seeing the new colleague. I hope we can help each other on the work.

I am free this weekend. How about having the dinner on Saturday night?

Yours sincerely,
Lily

亲爱的艾比：

收到你的来信我很开心。我很高兴你把你最好的朋友介绍给我，我很期待见到这位新同事。希望我们在以后的工作中能够相互帮助。

我这周末有时间，如果可以的话我们就定在这周六晚上一起吃个晚饭。

谨上！
莉莉

Dear Abby,

I am glad that you will introduce me a friend. I am willing to help her. But unfortunately, last week I had resigned, and now I am working in another company. I can't help her on the work, but you still can introduce her to me.

If possible, we can have dinner together tonight.

Yours sincerely,

Lily

亲爱的艾比：

你要给我介绍朋友我很高兴。我非常乐意帮助她，但是很遗憾，我上周已经辞职了，现在在另一家公司，所以不能在工作上给予帮助。但是你仍然可以把她介绍给我。

如果可以的话，今晚我们一起吃个饭。

谨上！

莉莉

范本二 | 介绍生意伙伴请求帮助

Dear Lily,

I need your help. One of my friends is eager to look for a business partner. I think you are the right person and able to help him. We have worked together for five years and are very familiar with each other. He is very clever and conversable. And he also keeps contact with many investment professionals. I believe that your cooperation will be very happy.

If you promise this, I will be very happy.

Yours sincerely,

Abby

亲爱的莉莉：

我需要你的帮助。我的一个朋友在正在急着寻找生意伙伴，我觉得你是能帮他的最佳人选。我和他在一起工作已经五年了，彼此都非常熟悉。他非常聪明，而且非常善于辞令，与很多投资人士都有联系。我相信你们会合作得很愉快的。

如果你答应，我会很高兴的。

谨上！

艾比

Dear Abby,

I am glad to receive your letter. After knowing some of his information from you, I am very glad to cooperate with him. If convenient, can you give me his number? I will contact him, and ask him something in detail.

I am very happy you can introduce such a good business partner to me. I will do my best to help him. I also hope that we can have a successful cooperation. Thank you.

Yours sincerely,

Lily

亲爱的艾比：

收到你的来信我很高兴。听你说了他的一些信息后，我非常乐意跟他合作。如果可以的话，能把他的联系方式给我吗？我会找个时间联系他，具体问问他一些事情。

非常高兴你能够介绍这么好的生意伙伴给我。我会尽我所能帮助他的。也希望我们的合作能够成功。谢谢你。

谨上！

莉莉

Dear Abby,

I'm glad you can introduce your good friend to me. I would like to work with him, but I have to know some specific matters to decide whether I can help him. If I am not good at his field, I may be incapable to do this.

Yours sincerely,

Lily

亲爱的艾比：

我很高兴你把你的好朋友介绍给我。我也非常想和他合作，但是我必须要知道一些具体事项才能知道我能否帮助他。如果他的领域我并不擅长，那我可能就无能为力了。

谨上！

莉莉

范本三 | 介绍职员请求帮助（1）

Dear Lily,

　　How are you recently? I write to introduce one of my staff to you. Don't worry. He is not fired for making mistakes. Actually I think his performance is very good, and he is good at communicating with others, sweet to customers. I think he is more suitable in the sales industry. So I would like to know if there is a suitable position in your company for him. I guarantee that he is a very diligent and hardworking person, and he will bring your company good performances. I hope you can consider this.

　　If you have any specific question or want to contact him, please call me. I hope you can think it over. Good luck!

Yours sincerely,
Abby

亲爱的莉莉：

　　最近还好吧？我想要把我的一个职员介绍给你。不要误会，他不是犯了什么错误被开除，相反我觉得他的表现很好，非常善于与人交流，能够非常贴心地为顾客服务，因此我觉得他更加适合在销售行业，所以我想看你们公司有没有适合他的职位。我保证他是个非常勤快和努力的人，一定会给你们公司带来业绩。希望你能考虑一下。

　　如果你还有什么具体的问题或是想要他的联系方式，请打电话给我。希望你能好好考虑一下。祝好运！

谨上！
艾比

Dear Abby,

　　Thank you for your letter. I'm glad you have such a good employee to introduce to me. After reading your letter, I think he is really suitable for our company. After discussion, we decide to hire him as a member of the sales department. I hope he will be able to have a good performance. And thank you very much for your introduction.

Yours sincerely,
Lily

亲爱的艾比：

　　谢谢你的来信。我很高兴你能把这么优秀的员工介绍给我。看过你的信以后，我觉得他确实很适合我们公司。经过讨论，我们决定聘用他到我们销售部工作，希望他以后好好表现。也非常感谢你的介绍。

谨上！
莉莉

Dear Abby,

　　I have received your letter. I know this employee must be very excellent. But I don't have the right to decide whether we can hire him, so I consulted the relevant departments, and decided not to hire him. If he wants to enter our corporation, he needs to come during the annual recruitment and go through the normal procedures of the company.

　　I'm sorry I can not help you. I hope I can see him in the recruiting. Thank you for your introduction.

Yours sincerely,
Lily

亲爱的艾比：

　　你的来信我已经收到。我想这名员工肯定非常出色，但是我没有权利决定是否能够雇用他，我咨询过有关部门后，决定不能录用他。他要想进入我们的公司需要通过每年招聘时期的正规程序。

　　我很抱歉没能够帮到你的忙，希望下次招聘的时候能够见到他。谢谢你的介绍。

谨上！
莉莉

范本四 | 介绍职员请求帮助（2）

Dear Lily,

　　Some bad news to tell you. Because of the financial crisis, my company has a cash flow problem, so I need to lay off employees. This decision is not easy for me. My employees are all very good.

　　I need your help. I would like to introduce you one of my staff. Although he has just joined the company for a few months, he is a quick-learner.His performance is also very good and he also gets along with the colleagues very well. I hope you can have a check to confirm if there is a suitable vacancy for him. I really hope that he can have a big growth in your company, and have a good future. I hope you can help me.

Yours sincerely,
Abby

亲爱的莉莉：

　　我要告诉你一个不幸的消息，由于金融危机的影响，我的公司资金周转不灵，需要裁员。这个决定对我来说非常艰难，我的员工都很优秀。

　　我需要你的帮助，我想向你介绍我的一名员工。他虽然刚进公司不久，但是他学习能力非常强，工作也非常出色，与同事们相处的非常好，所以我想把他介绍到你们公司任职。希望你可以帮我看看，你们公司是否有合适的空缺。我真的希望他能够在你们公司有所成长，能够有好的发展。希望你能够帮助我。

谨上！
艾比

Dear Abby,

　　I am sorry to hear that. If there is anything I can do to help you, please tell me. I think the employee you introduced is quite good. You can ask him to send a resume to me. I will discuss with the colleagues of the human resources department to see whether we can hire him. Don't worry. If he is really good, he will be warmly welcomed.

　　Wish you all the best!

Yours sincerely,
Lily

亲爱的艾比：

　　听到这个消息我很抱歉。如果有什么我能做的请告诉我。你介绍给我的这名员工我觉得非常不错，你可以让他发一份简历给我，我会和人力资源部的同事讨论一下看是否可以雇佣他。不用担心，如果他真的这么优秀我们非常欢迎他。

　　祝你一切顺利！

谨上！
莉莉

Dear Abby,

I am sorry to hear the difficulty that your company are facing. This financial crisis did bring a lot of problems to enterprises and cause a huge loss. Our company is also facing a lot of problems. Thank you very much for introducing me so excellent a staff. But I'm sorry, on the current tough situation, we are not planning to hire new employees.

Thank you for your introduction anyway. I'm sorry.

Yours sincerely,

Lily

亲爱的艾比：

听到你公司的问题我很抱歉。这场金融危机真的给很多企业都带来了巨大的损失，同样我们公司也面临着很多问题。非常感谢你能把这么优秀的员工介绍给我，但是我很抱歉，就目前艰难的情况来看，我们暂时不打算招聘新的员工。

但是还是很感谢你的推荐，很抱歉我没有帮上忙。

谨上！

莉莉

读书笔记

Lesson 9　祝贺信

如何写祝贺信

a 说明信息来源，开门见山表达自己的祝贺和喜悦。

b 对对方获得成就做出评价，肯定对方的努力，给予对方鼓励，也可以提出建议。

c 表达美好的祝愿。

实用例句

1. What exciting news!

   真是令人激动的消息！

2. I am so happy to hear this news!

   我很高兴听到这个消息。

3. It's the most joyful news I have heard for a long time.

   这是我这么长时间来听到的最令人高兴的消息。

4. Congratulations and best wishes to you.

   祝贺你，祝你一切都好。

5. You have done a good job, and I am so proud of you.

   你做得很好，我为你自豪。

6. You have paid a lot of efforts and you deserve it.

   你付出了很多努力，你值得拥有。

7. I will always be there for you. Keep going.

   我将永远在你身边支持你，继续努力。

8. I believe that you will make more achievements in your career.

   我相信你的事业将会有更多成就。

9. Wish you everything goes well!

   祝你一切顺利！

10. I hope you will have nothing but joy and happiness in your life.

    我希望你可以永远开心快乐。

范本一 | 祝贺升职

Dear Aaron,

I have just heard that you have been promoted to be the HR manager of your company. I am so happy that you get your promotion.

I was not surprised with this news, because you are the most diligent person in your department and willing to help everyone in your company. We all like you very much. And you always do excellent work, so you deserve it. I am sure you are qualified for this new job.

Wish you everything goes well!

Yours sincerely,

Tom

亲爱的艾伦：

我刚听说你升职为公司的人力资源主管，我非常开心听到你升职的消息。

我对你的升职并不惊讶，因为你是你们部门最勤奋的一个，乐于助人，我们都非常喜欢你。你的工作非常出色，这是你应得的职位。我相信你能胜任这个工作。

希望你一切都好！

汤姆谨上

Dear Tom,

I am so happy to hear from you. Thank you for your caring.

I really have paid a lot for this promotion. And I am very happy to have a payback. Experience in this process is precious. I will cherish it. And I will do my best on this position and will not let you down.

Wish you all the best!

Yours sincerely,

Aaron

亲爱的汤姆：

非常高兴收到你的来信，非常谢谢你的关心。

为了这个升职我真的付出了很多，很高兴现在有了收获。这个过程是人生难得的经历，我会好好珍惜它。我也会尽力做好这份工作，不辜负你的信任。

愿你一切都好！

艾伦谨上

Dear Tom,

Thank you very much for your concern. I'm glad I could get the promotion. But I think I still need to keep going. I will continue to work hard, and try my best to do the job. It will be a more difficult process. With your affirmation and encouragement, I believe I can do it. Let's do our best together.

Wish you healthy and work successfully!

Yours sincerely,

Aaron

亲爱的汤姆：

非常感谢你的关心。我很高兴我能够获得这次升职，但是我觉得自己还需要继续向前。我会继续努力，尽自己的能力把这个工作做好。这将会是一个更加艰辛的过程，但是有了你的肯定和鼓励，我相信我能做好。希望我们共同进步。

祝你身体健康，工作顺利！

艾伦谨上

范本二 | 祝贺乔迁

Dear Aaron,

I am glad to know you have moved to a better place. I am happy that you have owned better and beautiful surroundings. And I think you will have a wonderful life there.

It is your dream to have a house with a large garden, and because of your hard working, it comes true now. Congratulations. I have got your new address. I will visit you to see the new house soon.

I hope you will have nothing but joy and happiness in your life.

Yours sincerely,

Tom

亲爱的艾伦：

得知你们搬入了新家我很高兴。我为你们能够有更好更美的居住环境而开心。我想在那里你们将会有个很棒的生活。

拥有这样一个有大花园的房子一直是你的梦想。由于你的努力工作，这个梦想终于实现了。恭喜你。我已经有你的新地址，最近会去你的新家拜访并参观你们的新家。

希望你会有幸福美满的生活。

汤姆谨上

Dear Tom,

Thank you very much for your congratulations. I'm looking forward to your visit to my home.

As you said, the environment of my new home is very good. The roads are clean, the air is fresh, and the neighbors are very hospitable. We became friends a few days after we moved here. The facilities are very convenient. In a word, this is an ideal home. Welcome to my house.

Wish you all good!

Yours sincerely,

Aaron

亲爱的汤姆：

非常感谢你的祝贺。我非常期待你到我家来做客。

正如你所说的，我的新家环境非常好。马路很干净，周围空气清新，邻居们都很热情好客。没搬过来几天，我们就成了朋友。这里的设施也非常好。总之，这真是个理想中的家园。非常欢迎你来我家参观。

愿你一切都好！

艾伦谨上

Dear Tom,

Thank you for your concern. Our new home is quite good. The environment is beautiful and people here are hospitable. However, this place is far from the original school of the kids. It is not so convenient to pick up the kids. So I decide to let the children transfer to the school here. I think they'll quickly adapt to the new environment.

I am looking forward to your coming. I want to show you my big garden. I like it very much.

I wish you all the best!

Yours sincerely,

Aaron

亲爱的汤姆：

感谢你的关心。我们新家的确不错。这里环境优美，人们热情好客。但是，这里离孩子们原来的学校比较远。接送孩子们上下学不是很方便。所以我决定让孩子们转学。我觉得他们很快会适应这个新环境的。

非常期待你的到来。我很想让你看看我的大花园。我非常喜欢。

祝你一切都好！

艾伦谨上

范本三 | 祝贺订婚

Dear Aaron,

I have just heard that you will be engaged to the woman you love. It's the most joyful news I have heard for a long time. Congratulations and best wishes to you.

I think it is the most wonderful thing in the world. And from now on, you will have a fiancée who will love you and take care of you and be a part of your life. Life will be beautiful and happy with the women you love so much. I wish you can enjoy your life with her.

Allow me to offer my heartiest congratulations on your engagement.

Yours sincerely,

Tom

亲爱的艾伦：

我刚刚听说你和心爱的女人订婚的消息，这是我最近听到的最棒的喜讯。祝贺你订婚。

我想这应该是世界上最美好的事情。从现在开始，你将会有个爱你、照顾你的未婚妻，她会成为你生命中的一部分。和你爱的人一起，生活将会是美好和愉快的。我衷心地希望你和她能享受现在的生活。

允许我为你送上订婚最真挚的祝福。

汤姆谨上

Dear Tom,

Thank you for your blessing. I am very happy to receive the blessing from my best friend.

Lucy and I have been dating for three years before this day finally comes. I am very happy, very excited. I want to share my joy with you. You have witnessed our love. Thank you for your sincere blessing. We will be together forever.

May you find your love as soon as possible.

Yours sincerely,

Aaron

亲爱的汤姆：

　　非常感谢你的来信，谢谢你的祝福。我很高兴能够得到最好朋友的祝福。

　　我和露西交往了三年，这一天终于来了。我很开心，很激动，我很想和你一起分享这份喜悦。你见证了我们的爱情，谢谢你真挚的祝福，我们会永不分离。

　　愿你也早日找到自己的另一半。

艾伦谨上

Dear Tom,

　　I am more than happy to receive your letter. Thank you for your blessing.

　　Engaged to the person I love is really happy. Thank you for your always concerning. I hope you can come to our engagement ceremony. I hope that I can start a new life with the company of my best friend.

　　I am looking forward to your coming. Wish you all the best!

Yours sincerely,
Aaron

亲爱的汤姆：

　　非常高兴收到你的来信。谢谢你的祝福。

　　能够与自己所爱的人订婚真是一件幸福的事情，感谢你一直以来的关心，希望你能来我们的订婚典礼。我衷心希望能够在我最好朋友的陪伴下迎接新的生活。

　　期待你的到来。祝你一切都好！

艾伦谨上

范本四 | 祝贺新婚

Dear Aaron,

　　It's wonderful to know that you have married the woman you love. From now on, you will start a family and live a happy life with your wife.

　　You are born of a couple. For so many years, you have been loving each other, come over many difficulties and challenges and finally get together. It is really wonderful. And you should tolerate each other and take care of each other in the coming days. Wish you all the best.

　　Allow me to offer my heartiest congratulations on your marriage.

Yours sincerely,
Tom

亲爱的艾伦：

　　非常高兴听到你和心爱的人结婚的消息。现在开始你将建立一个新的家庭，将会和你的妻子过上美好的生活。

　　你们是天造地设的一对。这么多年来，你们彼此相爱，克服了很多的苦难和挑战，现在终于能够携手在一起，这是多么美好的事情。希望在未来的日子你们能够相互包容，相互关爱。祝你们一切都好。

　　允许我为你们的新婚送上最真挚的祝福。

汤姆谨上

Dear Tom,

　　I feel so happy to receive your letter of blessing.

　　This process is long and happy, both exciting and nervous. Marriage is the most wonderful thing in one's life. I have already prepared to begin a new life with my wife. We will care about each other, tolerate each other. Thank you for your support and blessing. It is precious to us.

　　I wish you in good health and have a happy life!

Yours sincerely,
Aaron

亲爱的汤姆：

　　能收到你的来信祝福，我是多么的幸福。

　　这个过程是漫长而幸福的，既兴奋又紧张。结婚是人生中最美好的事情，我已经做好准备和我的妻子迎接一个新的生活。我们会相互关心，互相包容。感谢你对我们结婚的支持和祝福，这对我们来说非常珍贵。

　　祝你身体健康，生活愉快！

艾伦谨上

Dear Tom,

　　Thank you very much for your letter of blessing. My wife and I are both very happy to receive your blessing on the wedding.

　　I am still very excited. I can't believe that I have married the women I love. I know this means I will take on the responsibility of a family, and I should love and protect my family. I believe that I can be a good husband and a good father. Thank you for your advice and blessing.

　　I wish you all the best!

Yours sincerely,
Aaron

亲爱的汤姆:

非常感谢你的来信祝福。收到你对我们的结婚祝福我和我妻子都非常高兴。

我的心情至今还非常激动，真不敢相信我已经和我最爱的女人结婚了。我知道这意味着我将会要承担起一个家的责任，需要爱护和保护我的家庭。我相信我能成为一个好丈夫，一个好爸爸。谢谢你的建议和祝福。

祝你一切都好!

艾伦谨上

范本五 | 祝贺添丁

Dear Aaron,

I am delighted to hear that you are now a father. The best thing in the world is to have a child to see the continuation of life.

Your baby must be very lovely and wish him to grow healthily and happily. And from now on, you will have more responsibilities and expectations. Your wife is a very great woman. Help me to send my wishes to your wife. You are a lucky man to have these two persons.

Wish you have a wonderful life!

Yours sincerely,

Tom

亲爱的艾伦:

我很高兴听到你终于做爸爸了。世界上最美好的是莫过于有自己的孩子，看到自己生命的延续。

我想你的宝宝一定很可爱，希望她健康快乐地成长。从现在起，你将多一份责任，也多一份期望。你的妻子真了不起，代我向你妻子表达祝福。能够拥有这两个人，你真是个幸运的男人。

希望你有美好的生活!

汤姆谨上

Dear Tom,

I am very glad to receive your blessing. Being a father is really a fantastic thing. My heart is full of sweet ness.

I know that raising a child need to pay a lot, but I am really looking forward to seeing the growth of the baby. This must be a very happy thing. My baby really brings us a lot of joy.

Thank you for the blessing to my baby. Wish you a happy life!

Yours sincerely,

Aaron

亲爱的汤姆：

非常高兴收到你的祝福。做爸爸真是一种神奇的感觉，觉得自己心里充满了甜蜜。

我知道养育一个孩子需要付出很多，但是却非常期待能够看着孩子一点点的成长。我想这将会是一件非常开心的事情。孩子真的带给了我们很多快乐。

谢谢你对孩子的祝福。祝你生活愉快！

艾伦谨上

Dear Tom,

I am very pleased to receive your letter. Thank you for your blessing to our children.

Being a father for the first time, I feel very happy and excited as well as a bit of nervous. It is very difficult to take care of and raise a child. We have a lot of things to learn. Although it is very hard, I still feel very happy. I think this is the feeling of being a dad. I'll become a good husband and father.

Wish you a happy life, and wish you all the best!

Yours sincerely,

Aaron

亲爱的汤姆：

非常高兴收到你的来信，谢谢你对我们和孩子的祝福。

初为人父，让我感到非常的高兴和兴奋，但是同时也有点儿不知所措。我发现要很好地照顾和抚养孩子是一件非常困难的事情，我们有很多东西需要学习。照顾宝宝虽然辛苦，但是我的心里却是非常甜蜜，我想这就是做爸爸的感觉。我会成为一个好丈夫和好爸爸的。

也祝你生活开心！一切都好！

艾伦谨上

范本六 | 祝贺获胜

Dear Aaron,

I am writing to convey my congratulations on your success on the tennis tournament. I am happy that your hard work and genius have been rewarded.

You have prepared for this tournament for a long time, an have practiced very hard. I think you deserve it. I am so proud of you. Maybe we should have a dinner together to talk all about this game to share your happiness. And I am looking forward to hearing more good news about your games.

Congratulations and best wishes to you.

Yours sincerely,

Tom

亲爱的艾伦：

祝贺你在网球锦标赛上获得成功。我很高兴你的才能和勤奋得到了回报。

你为了这个比赛准备了相当长的一段时间，练习得非常勤奋，我想这是你应得的，我为你感到骄傲。也许我们需要约个时间把酒言欢，好好谈论这场比赛，分享你的喜悦。我期待听到更多你比赛的好消息。

恭喜你，也祝福你。

汤姆谨上

Dear Tom,

Thank you for your praise and congratulations. I am also looking forward to meeting you and sharing my experience with you.

Best wishes!

Yours sincerely,

Aaron

亲爱的汤姆：

非常谢谢你的肯定和祝贺。我也非常期待和你分享一下我的比赛经历。

祝好！

艾伦谨上

Dear Tom,

Thank you for your congratulations. I am very happy to win. Thanks for your encouragement. I will make persistent efforts, to gain a bigger victory. I will do more practice in the following days. I'm very happy to share the game process with you.

Best wishes!

Yours sincerely,

Aaron

亲爱的汤姆：

谢谢你的来信祝贺。能够获得胜利我非常开心，也谢谢你的鼓励，我会再接再厉，争取获得更大的胜利。接下来的日子里我会更加努力地练习。我非常乐意与你分享这个比赛的过程。

祝好！

艾伦谨上

范本七 | 祝贺金榜题名

Dear Aaron,

I am so happy to hear the news that you have recieved the admission to the ×××University. And in September, you will be a college student in your dreaming university. I am so excited about it.

You are always the best in your class, and I was not so surprised about this news. But I was really happy to hear this. I think your hard work and intelligence have been recognized by the school. Wish you have a good school life and be the best as before.

Congratulations on your admission. I believe you will make more achivements in the college.

Yours sincerely,

Tom

亲爱的艾伦：

得知你已经被×××大学录取的消息我很高兴。九月，你将成为你梦想大学的一名学生，我很高兴。

你总是班级里成绩最好的，我对你被录取的消息不是很惊讶，但是真的非常高兴。我想你的勤奋和聪慧得到了这所大学的认可，希望你有个美好的大学生活，也能像平时一样成为最好的学生。

恭喜你收到录取通知书，我相信你在大学里能获得更多成就。

汤姆谨上

Dear Tom,

Thank you for your letter of congratulations. I am very happy to enter the dreaming university. I'm longing for the college life. Although I don't know what I will experience, I believe that I can do everything well just like now. Thanks for your encouragement. Hope you can also receive good news.

Bless you!

Yours sincerely,

Aaron

亲爱的汤姆：

谢谢你的来信祝贺。能够进入这个梦想的大学，我真的非常高兴。我对大学生活充满了向往，虽然不知道我会经历什么，但是我相信我能像现在一样做好每件事。非常谢谢你对我的鼓励，希望你也能收到好消息。

祝福你！

艾伦谨上

Dear Tom,

Thank you very much for your concern. I'm very happy to be able to enter the dreaming university. I have made many plans. I want to join in the student union, get a lot of scholarships, and take part in all kinds of activities. I want to have a full and rich university life. I'm looking forward to the college life. Wish you can have a good university life too.

Bless you!

Yours sincerely,

Aaron

亲爱的汤姆：

非常感谢你的关心。我很高兴能够进入梦想的大学，我对大学做了很多规划，我想在大学里加入学生会，想得奖学金，想要参加各种活动。我想把大学生活过得丰富充实，我非常期待大学生活，同样也祝你能够有个美好的大学生活。

祝福你！

艾伦谨上

范本八 | 祝贺毕业

Dear Aaron,

　　Congratulations on your graduation. After four-year life in the university, I believe that you have learned a lot of knowledge and gained much experience. This period of time will be your best memory.

　　You will have a new job and a new life. I'm glad you will begin your new journey. Don't be sad about the separation from your friends and teachers. Everyone will have a better future. Let's cheer for the future together.

　　As your friend, I am happy for your beginning of a new life. I hope you will gain more success.

Yours sincerely,

Tom

亲爱的艾伦：

　　恭喜你毕业了。经过了四年的大学生活，相信你收获了很多知识和经验，这段时间的生活将会成为你一生最美好的记忆。

　　接下来你将要迎接新工作和新生活。很高兴你将开始你人生一段新的旅程。不要伤感与朋友和老师的分别，大家都会有美好的未来，一起为我们未来加油喝彩吧。

　　作为你的朋友，我为你将开始新生活感到高兴。希望你以后会收获更多成功。

汤姆谨上

Dear Tom,

　　Thank you for your letter. After four years of studying, we will go out of the campus, and enter the society. I think we have to overcome a lot of difficulties and challenges in future. I believe that as long as I work hard, I will have a bright future. I hope we can work hard together, and create a good life belonging to ourselves.

　　I wish you all the best.

Yours sincerely,

Aaron

亲爱的汤姆：

　　谢谢你的来信。经过四年的学习，我们终于要走出校园，走入社会，未来有很多困难和挑战等着我们去克服。我相信只要努力，我一定会有个美好的未来。希望我们共同努力，创造属于我们的生活。

　　祝你一切顺利！

艾伦谨上

Dear Tom,

　　Thank you for your congratulations. I feel very excited and nervous to get out of the campus. I am so excited to the future but also not so sure about it. To separate with my dear friends and teachers makes me so sad. But I believe that we can all have a bright future by our own efforts.

　　With best wishes for every success!

Yours sincerely,
Aaron

亲爱的汤姆：

　　谢谢你的祝贺。要走出校园，我感到非常的兴奋和紧张。对未来我充满着向往，但是又有不确定。要与亲爱的朋友和老师离别也让我很感伤，但是我相信，凭我们自己的努力我们都能闯出一片天。

　　祝你一切顺利！

艾伦谨上

范本九 | 祝贺生日

Dear Aaron,

　　Today is your 20th birthday and happy birthday!

　　Twenty years ago, you came to the world. You are a kind, hard-working person who always concern about your friends and enjoy life. I'm very lucky to be your friend. Please accept my sincere wishes. And I have a small gift for you, and hope you like it.

　　Happy birthday to you!

Yours sincerely,
Tom

亲爱的艾伦：

今天是你二十岁的生日，祝你生日快乐！

二十年前，你来到这个世界。你是个善良、勤奋的人，关心朋友、热爱生活，我很幸运能有你这个朋友，请收下我最真挚的祝福。我有份小礼物要送给你，希望你喜欢。

生日快乐，我的朋友！

汤姆谨上

Dear Tom,

Thank you for your birthday wishes. I am very happy to receive your letter on my birthday. Each year my parents and so many friends will come to celebrate birthday for me. I really feel very happy.

Bless you!

Yours sincerely,

Aaron

亲爱的汤姆：

谢谢你的生日祝福。我很高兴能够在生日的时候收到你的来信。每次生日都有我的父母和这么多朋友为我庆祝，我真的非常幸福。

祝福你！

艾伦谨上

Dear Tom,

Thank you for your gift. I like it very much. I am very lucky to have so many friends to accompany by my side. I hope everyone around me be happy every day, and this is my birthday wish.

With all good wishes!

Yours sincerely,

Aaron

亲爱的汤姆：

谢谢你送我礼物，我很喜欢。我很庆幸能有这么多朋友陪伴在我的身边。我希望身边的每个人每天都开开心心，这就是我的生日愿望。

祝你顺心如意！

艾伦谨上

范本十 | 祝贺周年

Dear Aaron,

Congratulations on the thirty anniversaries of your company. As your friend, I have witnessed the growth of the company, and know that each staff has paid a lot. I really admire your efforts and pay.

Now it is growing rapidly. The scale of the company is expanding. It is in a good position in this industry. More and more people get to know more and more about the products. Although there were many crisis and challenges, you had overcome all of them. It's like your child, becoming better under your good caring. I hope you can continue to work hard to gain greater success!

Yours sincerely,

Tom

亲爱的艾伦：

恭喜你的公司建立三十周年。作为你的朋友，我见证这个公司的成长以及每位员工对它的付出。我非常敬佩你们的努力和付出。

现在的它正处于快速成长时期。公司的规模在不断扩大，在这个行业也取得了很好的地位，人们对于产品也越来越熟知。虽然也有过危机和挑战，但是你都克服了。它就像你的孩子，在你精心照顾下，成长得越来越好。希望你们能够继续努力，获得更大的成功！

汤姆谨上

Dear Tom,

Thank you for your letter. It has been thirty years since I set up the company, and it feels like yesterday. During so many years, I have got a lot of experience and feelings here. I appreciate my employees and my family members. I have got so much support from them. And I also appreciate my dear friends. In this process, you give me a lot of advice and encouragement. I really appreciate your help.

Bless you!

Yours sincerely,

Aaron

亲爱的汤姆：

　　谢谢你的来信。转眼三十多年过去了，想到当初刚刚建立它的时候，就像是在昨天。经过这么多年，在这里获得了很多经验和感受。我非常感谢我的员工和家人对我的支持，同样也感谢我亲爱的朋友。在这个过程中你给了我很多建议和鼓励，非常感谢你对我的帮助。

　　祝福你！

艾伦谨上

Dear Tom,

　　Thank you very much for your letter, for your care about my company.

　　As you said, it is like my kid. Today is its 30 anniversary and I am so happy about it. I think I should work harder to make it grow more rapidly. I should thank my employees for so many years' hard work. We are like a big family, loving each other. Every staff will be proud of it.

　　Thank you for your affirmation and encouragement. Those help me a lot. Thank you.

　　I wish you all the best!

Yours sincerely,
Aaron

亲爱的汤姆：

　　非常感谢你的来信，非常感谢你对我公司的关心。

　　正如你说的它就像是我的孩子一样，公司三十周年生日让我非常高兴。我想我还需要更加努力，让它能更加快速地成长。我非常感谢这期间员工的付出，我们就像一个大家庭一样，相亲相爱，每位员工都将以它为傲。

　　这期间谢谢你对我肯定和鼓励，这对我帮助很大。很感谢你。

　　祝你一切顺利！

艾伦谨上

范本十一 | 祝贺开业

Dear Aaron,

　　Congratulations on the opening ceremony of your clothing store. I'm glad you became a boss to work for yourself.

Opening a clothing store is also a hard thing. You need to understand a lot of clothing knowledge, know much about the market, and so on. I believe you have spent a lot of time and energy opening the store. I really admire that you have the courage to give up a stable job, and to do what you like. Most of the people can't do it. If you need, please contact me, I will do my best to help you.

I wish you all the best!

Yours sincerely,

Tom

亲爱的艾伦：

恭喜你的服装店开张。我很高兴你现在成了为自己工作的老板。

开服装店也是一件辛苦的事情，你需要了解很多服装知识，了解市场等等。我相信你为了开这个店花了很多时间和精力，我真的很佩服你的勇气，能够放弃一份稳定的工作，做自己想做的事情，这不是很多人能做到的。如果你有需要，请联系我，我会尽我所能帮助你。

祝你一切顺利！

汤姆谨上

Dear Tom,

Thank you for your congratulations. And also thank you for your willingness to help me. Opening the clothing store is indeed a hard thing, but I am very happy and enjoyable. Now what I am doing is my dream. I think doing what I am interested in is a wonderful thing. Hope it will be better and better in the future.

Also bless you!

Yours sincerely,

Aaron

亲爱的汤姆：

非常感谢你的祝贺，也非常感谢你愿意帮助我。开这个服装店的确是件不容易的事情，但是我很快乐，很享受。我现在做的事情正是我的梦想，能够做自己感兴趣的事情，是一件非常快乐的事情。希望未来越来越好！

也祝福你！

艾伦谨上

Dear Tom,

Thank you for your letter. I'm glad to hear that you are willing to help me. I really have a lot of problems to solve and I need help from others. You know I am not a master of this field, and I need to learn many things. But I have confidence that as long as I want to do it, I can do it well. I hope you can give me more advices. I can't thank you more.

Wish you happy every day!

Yours sincerely,

Aaron

亲爱的汤姆：

谢谢你的来信。很高兴听你说你愿意帮助我，我的确有很多问题需要别人的帮助。你知道我并不是这方面的专家，需要学习很多东西。但是我有信心，只要我想做，一定能做好。希望你能给我更多建议，我感激不尽。

祝你天天开心！

艾伦谨上

范本十二 | 祝贺当选

Dear Aaron,

Congratulations on your election as president of the student union of the school. Everyone has witnessed what you have done for a long time. You have excellent performance, are willing to help others, and also have organized many activities. These things show us that you possess strong leadership and communication capacity. We all think that you can do the job well. We hope you can think and do more for the students after election. I also believe that you can do it excellently, and will meet our expectation.

Hope to hear more good news from you!

Yours sincerely,

Tom

亲爱的艾伦：

祝贺你当选学校的学生会主席一职。长久以来你的努力，大家都看得见。你成绩优秀，乐于帮助同学，组织了多项活动，表现出了很强的领导能力，沟通能力，我们都认为你能够胜任这个工作。希望你当上学生会主席后能够更好地为学生谋福利，办实事。我也相信你能够做好，不会辜负我们大家对你的期望。

希望能够听到你更多好消息！

汤姆谨上

Dear Tom,

Thank you for your encouragement. I am very happy that you believe in me. I will work harder.

To become the president of the student union is my goal in my school life. I am willing to know the thoughts of students, and communicate with the teachers, hoping to get more information and power for our students to have a good school life here. During the process I also learned a lot of things. When I become the president of the student union, I'll learn to know more about the job and serve for the students. Thank you for your support.

Thank you for your congratulations. Also bless you!

Yours sincerely,

Aaron

亲爱的汤姆：

谢谢你的来信鼓励。我非常高兴你们能够相信我，我会更加努力的。

一直以来我都以成为学生会主席为目标。我积极了解同学们的想法，和老师进行沟通，希望为同学们取得更多信息和权利，让同学们在这儿有一份美好的学校生活。这个过程中我也学习到了很多东西，成为学生会主席后，我会更加全面地了解这个工作，更好地为同学们服务。非常感谢你们的支持。

谢谢你的祝贺，也祝福你！

艾伦谨上

Dear Tom,

Thank you for your congratulations. It was your support that made me elected as the president of the student union. I will not let you down. I will provide better service for students.

The job of president of the student union is very heavy. I think it is not enough to count on myself, and also need to corporate with all the members of the school union. Only through the team efforts can we better develop the school union and work for the student. Thanks for your encouragement and support.

I wish you all the best!

Yours sincerely,

Aaron

亲爱的汤姆：

谢谢你的祝贺。我能够当选学生会主席都是因为你的支持，我不会让你们失望，我会更好地为学生服务。

学生会主席的工作任务非常繁重，我觉得依靠我自己一个人的力量肯定是不够的，我还需要与学生会各个成员更好地合作，只有团队努力才能让学生会更好地发展。同时谢谢你对我的鼓励和支持。

祝你一切顺利！

艾伦谨上

范本十三 | 祝贺表扬

Dear Aaron,

I'm glad your composition got the first prize in the national essay contest and you have received the praise from the Principal. I have read your article. It is really great. The composition is very smooth, and the sentences are very beautiful. It has profound educational significance that lead us to think more about life. I think it is a matter of course that this article obtains the national first prize. The praise of the school also makes it more famous. Many students have read it and like it very much.

I admire you can write such a good article. Hope you can continue to work hard, and write more and better articles to win the honor for our school. I'm very proud of you.

Yours sincerely,

Tom

亲爱的艾伦：

我很高兴你的作文得了全国一等奖，收到了校长的表扬。我已经读过你的文章了，觉得你写得非常好。文章很流畅，语句也很美，有很深刻的教育意义，让我们更多地思考生活。我觉得这篇文能够获得全国一等奖是理所当然的。学校的表扬也让你的文章变得更加有名，很多同学读了以后都很喜欢这篇文章。

　　我很钦佩你能够写出这么好的文章，希望你能够继续努力，写出更多更好的文章，为学校赢得荣誉。我很为你自豪。

汤姆谨上

Dear Tom,

　　Thank you for your congratulations and praise. I feel very happy to receive praise from the school. What makes me more pleased is that you all like my article. I feel very satisfied and proud. Thank you for your support.

　　My work inspiration is mainly from my life, and I think as a student, we need to think a lot about the meaning of life. I just write down what I think and express my feelings. Unexpectedly, it can be recognized by so many people. I'll work harder and write more works for you to read.

　　Thank you very much for your support. Bless you!

Yours sincerely,
Aaron

亲爱的汤姆：

　　谢谢你的祝贺和赞美。能够得到学校的表扬，我觉得非常高兴，但是更开心的是你们都喜欢我的作品，我感到很满足，很自豪。谢谢你们的支持。

　　我的作品主要灵感来源于我的生活，我觉得作为一个学生需要思考很多有关人生意义的话题。我只是把我想到的表达出来，但没想到却能够得到大家的认同，我会更加努力，争取写出更多作品让大家欣赏。

　　非常感谢你的支持，祝福你！

艾伦谨上

Dear Tom,

　　Thank you for your congratulations. I am very glad you like it.

　　The main purpose to write is to let readers think, and get something. I think my article did it. I'm very happy and proud. But I'll work harder to express what I think from every angle to express my feelings and sentiment. I also hope more people will be able to get some thoughts from my article. Thank you very much for your praise. And I will have stronger motivation to continue my writing.

Thank you very much. Bless you!

Yours sincerely,
Aaron

亲爱的汤姆：

　　谢谢你的祝贺，很高兴你们都喜欢它。

　　我想写作的主要目的就是想让读者有所思考并获取一些东西，我想我的这篇文章做到了。我很高兴，很自豪，但我会更加努力，从各个方面更好地诠释我想要表达的感想和感悟，也希望有更多人能够从我的文章中得到一些思考。非常感谢你的赞美，你们的肯定使我更有动力继续我的写作。

　　非常感谢你，祝福你！

艾伦谨上

范本十四 | 祝贺演讲

Dear Aaron,

　　Congratulations on your successful speech. Yesterday I listened to your lecture about the "Relation Between Environment and Human", and benefited a lot. Your discussion was simple but deep and rich in content. They well showed the relation between environment and human beings. You pointed out many questions. And you also came up with some environmental problems that human beings are going to be faced with in the future. Then you put forward your own views. I found all the audience heard very carefully and everyone gave your speech praise. I think your lecture is very successful.

　　I'm looking forward to your next brilliant speech. Best wishes!

Yours sincerely,
Tom

亲爱的艾伦：

　　祝贺你的演讲获得了成功。我昨天听了你《环境与人类的关系》的讲座，受益匪浅。你的论述浅显易懂，内容丰富，很好的说明了当前环境与人类的关系。指出了很多值得深思的问题，也看到了未来人类将面临的环境问题，并提出了自己的观点。我发现观众们都听得非常认真，大家对你的演讲都赞不绝口。我认为你的讲座非常的成功。

我期待你更多精彩的演讲，祝福你！

汤姆谨上

Dear Tom,

Thank you for your congratulations. I'm glad that you came to listen to my lecture. I really want to hear your opinions on the subject and I hope we can make an appointment to discuss this topic. Thank you for your letter.

I wish you healthy and happy!

Yours sincerely,

Aaron

亲爱的汤姆：

非常感谢你的来信祝贺。我很高兴你来听我的讲座，我非常想听听你对这个话题的想法，希望我们可以约个时间深入探讨一下这个话题。感谢你的来信。

祝你身体健康，生活愉快！

艾伦谨上

Dear Tom,

Thank you for your letter. I'm glad you give such high evaluation on my lecture. I think the topic about relation between environment and human beings is a hot global topic, and we can talk much about it. I am eager to talk with others about this topic. If you would like to, I hope we can set a time for a discussion. I think your thoughts will give me more enlightenment.

Thank you! I wish you all the best!

Yours sincerely,

Aaron

亲爱的汤姆：

感谢你的来信，我很高兴你对我的讲座给了这么高的评价。我觉得环境与人类关系的话题是个全球热点的话题，是个广泛讨论的问题，我非常期待能和别人一起探讨这个话题。如果你愿意的话，我希望能跟你定个时间讨论一下这个话题。我想你的思想一定能给我更多的启示。

谢谢！祝你一切顺利！

艾伦谨上

Lesson 10　慰问信

如何写慰问信

ⓐ 首先表示自己的慰问，给予对方理解和鼓励。

ⓑ 如果可能的话，告知能够让对方高兴和振作的消息，来帮助其恢复精神。

ⓒ 表达自己的美好祝愿，希望对方早日康复。

实用例句

1. I am sorry to hear that you had a bad cold. I know a cold always companies with nasal congestion, runny nose and sneezing, so you must feel very uncomfortable.

听到你得了重感冒的消息我很抱歉，我知道感冒经常会伴随着鼻塞、流鼻涕和打喷嚏的症状，这十分难受。

2. I know how it feels and I can totally understand what you are suffering. I hope you can soon recover.

我知道这个感受，我能了解你的痛苦，我希望你可以快点康复。

3. I feel so lonely without you going with me for this trip, because you have a bad cold. But don't worry. I will bring beautiful photos for you about the trip.

因为你得重感冒不能和我一起来旅行，我感到很孤单，但是不用担心，我会多带点好看的照片给你。

4. I am so sorry for your loss. I want you to know I will always be here with you and support you.

对于你的损失，我很抱歉。我想让你知道我会一直在这里陪着你，支持你。

5. I was shocked by the news that you had a car accident last night. You must be frightened too.

听到你昨晚出车祸的消息我很震惊，你也一定被吓到了。

6. I am so sorry to know that there was an earthquake in your city. Please take care of yourself and call me anytime.

听到你住的城市发生了地震的消息我很难过，请照顾好你自己，随时打电话给我。

7. I saw the news on TV about the fire and I am so sad to hear that the buildings were all burnt in the fire, but I rejoice that you didn't get hurt.

我在电视上看到了关于这场火灾的消息，听到房子烧毁的消息我很难过，但是我很高兴你没有受伤。

8. I am so sorry to hear that your family have suffered a devastating flood. But I think the most important thing is that you are all fine. And I hope you can get through this and I will try my best to help you.

听到你们家受到了洪水的袭击我很难过，但是我认为最重要的是你们都安全。我希望你们能够度过这个艰难的时刻，我会尽我所能帮助你们。

9. I haven't seen you for a long time. I hope everything is OK. And I want to pay a visit to you this weekend.

我很久没有见到您了，希望您一切都好，这周末我会来看望您。

10. Best wishes for you. I really hope you can be better and see you soon.

在这里送上我最真诚的祝福。我真的希望你可以恢复，希望能尽快见到你。

范本一 | 生病慰问（1）

Dear White,

　　I am sorry to hear that you had a bad cold. I know a cold always companies with nasal congestion, runny nose and sneezing. You must feel very uncomfortable. I know how it feels and I can totally understand what you are suffering. You should drink more water and take the pills on time. I hope you can soon recover. Then we can go for a travel to Hainan and have a wonderful time.

　　Best wishes!

Yours sincerely,
Lucy

亲爱的怀特：

　　听到你得了重感冒的消息我很难过，我知道感冒经常会伴随着鼻塞、流鼻涕和打喷嚏的症状，这十分难受。我知道这个感受，我能了解你的痛苦。你应该多喝水，按时吃药。我希望你可以快点康复，这样我们就可以一起去海南旅行，度过一个美好的假期。

　　祝好！

露西谨上

Dear Lucy,

Thank you for your letter. I am looking forward to this travel which we have planned for a long time. I will take your advice and take care of myself. So I can get better soon and go for the travel.

Thank you for your wishes!

Yours sincerely,

White

亲爱的露西：

谢谢你的来信，我很期待我们计划了很久的这个旅行。我会遵照你的建议，好好照顾自己，争取快点恢复，这样我们就能按计划去旅行了。

谢谢你的祝福！

怀特谨上

Dear Lucy,

I am so sorry that because of my cold we couldn't go travelling as soon as possible. And I will take care of myself. If you want to go first, it is OK with me. And I will go there later. Thus you can know much about the place and take me around.

Best wishes!

Yours sincerely,

White

亲爱的露西：

我很抱歉，因为我的感冒，我们不能尽早去旅行。我会照顾好我自己的，如果你想要先过去的话，我同意，我可以晚点过去。这样你就可以好好地先了解一下当地的情况，随后可以带我好好逛逛。

祝好！

怀特谨上

范本二 | 生病慰问（2）

Dear White,

I am sorry to hear that you have a fever and can't come to the class. These days you have been busy with a lot of things. You not only helped the teacher do the project, but also managed the affairs of the class and participated in several activities. You didn't have enough time to eat or rest. You should look after yourself. I hope you can be better soon, so we can study together again. We all miss you very much.

Best wishes!

Yours sincerely,
Lucy

亲爱的怀特：

听说你发烧不能来上课，我很难过。这些日子你一直在忙着做很多事情，既要帮助老师做项目，又要管理班级，还要参加各种活动，你几乎没有怎么好好吃饭和休息，你要好好照顾自己，希望你赶快康复，这样我们又能在一起学习。我们都很想你。

祝好！

露西谨上

Dear Lucy,

I am glad to hear this. Thank you for your greetings. I will be fine soon and return to school. If it is convenient for you, please tell the teacher that I will come back the day after tomorrow. Hope to see you soon.

Best wishes!

Yours sincerely,
White

亲爱的露西：

我很高兴收到你的来信，谢谢你的问候。我会很快就恢复，回学校。如果你方便的话，请帮我告诉老师一声，我会在后天回学校。期待立刻见到你们。

祝好！

怀特谨上

Dear Lucy,

I'm very pleased to receive your letter. I miss you too. But my temperature is still high, so I should go to the hospital to have a check. I might not be able to go back to school recently. If it is possible, please contact with me every day, and tell me what happens in school. It would give me so much fun.

Best wishes!

Yours sincerely,
White

亲爱的露西：

我很高兴收到你的来信，我也很想念你们。但是由于我的体温一直很高，要入院检查，所以短期内，我可能没有办法回学校。如果可以的话，请每天跟我联系，告诉我学校发生的一些事情，这样会让我好过一点。

祝好！

怀特谨上

范本三 | 慰问长辈健康

Dear Grandma,

Long time no see. How is everything going? A few days ago, I heard that you had a little cold. I hope you feel better now. Recently I am busy with my study, so I don't have much time to see you. I am so sorry about this. I will visit you this weekend and then we can go for a walk and have a big meal together. Hope to see you soon. And promise me that you will take good care of yourself.

Best wishes!

Yours sincerely,

Lucy

亲爱的外婆：

很久没见，最近好吗？前几天听说你有点感冒，希望你已经好了。最近我忙着学习的事情，所以没时间去看你，我很抱歉。我会在这周末去看你，我们可以一起散个步，吃个饭。希望赶快见到你，也希望你答应我要好好照顾自己。

祝好！

露西谨上

Dear Lucy,

I am happy to hear from you. I feel better now and there is nothing wrong with my body. I am looking forward to your coming. I will prepare your favorite dishes.

Love you!

Yours sincerely,

Grandma

亲爱的露西：

　　收到你的来信我很高兴。我的感冒已经好了，身体也很好。期待你的到来，我将会为你准备你最爱吃的菜。

　　爱你！

外婆

Dear Lucy,

　　I am so happy to hear that you will come. I know you are busy with your study, and it is your most important thing. If you don't have time to come for a visit, I can understand. And I am in good health now, so don't worry about me.

　　Love you!

Yours sincerely,
Grandma

亲爱的露西：

　　我很高兴听到你要来的消息。我知道你最近学习很忙，学习是最重要的事情，如果你没有时间来看望我，我能理解。现在我的身体很好，不用担心我。

　　爱你！

外婆

范本四 | 车祸慰问

Dear White,

　　I was shocked to hear that you had a car accident last night. You must be frightened too. Fortunately, you are not seriously injured. I don't know if this thing will affect your life, but if you need to talk, please give me a call. I would like to share your feelings. You know people will always experience some terrible things, and we must learn to forget. Hope you can recover quickly. We will help you at your side.

　　Best wishes!

Yours sincerely,
Lucy

亲爱的怀特：

　　听到你昨晚出车祸的消息我很震惊，你也一定被吓到了。很庆幸，你没有受什么大的伤。不知道这件事情会对你造成什么影响，如果你需要聊聊的话，就打给我，我愿意分享你的感受。要知道谁都会经历一些可怕的事情，我们必须学会忘记。希望你能赶快恢复，我们都会在你身边帮助你。

祝好！

露西谨上

Dear Lucy,

It is so sweet of you to give me this letter. I feel much better now and I can read your care and wishes. Thank you very much. I will be fine soon, and don't worry about me.

Best wishes!

Yours sincerely,
White

亲爱的露西：

你的这封信让我感到很贴心。我已经好多了，我能从信中读到你的关心和祝福，非常谢谢你。我会很快恢复，不要担心我。

祝好！

怀特谨上

Dear Lucy,

It's very kind of you. This accident does make me feel scared. Sometimes I still wake up with a start by nightmare. Survived the disaster, I feel very lucky. I'm glad you can write to me and give me encouragement. I will try to overcome the fear. With your encouragement, I believe I'll recover soon.

Best wishes!

Yours sincerely,
White

亲爱的露西：

你人真好。这次的车祸的确让我感到害怕，我有时候还是会在梦中惊醒。能够躲过这次的劫难，我觉得很幸运，我很高兴你能够写信来给我鼓励，我将会努力克服恐惧。有了你们的鼓励，我相信我会很快恢复的。

祝好！

怀特谨上

范本五 | 火灾慰问

Dear White,

I am sorry to hear that your house was on fire last night. I know you have lost a lot of things, because the house was burnt to the ground. Fortunately, you were not hurt. I think life is more important than anything else. Only when you are alive can you create wealth. Don't worry. You still have us, and we will help you and support you. As long as we unite together, we can get through the difficulties. Hope that you can snap out of it.

Best wishes!

Yours sincerely,

Lucy

亲爱的怀特：

听到你们家昨晚发生火灾的消息我很难过。我知道你们失去了很多东西，房子被烧毁了，东西也都被烧光了。但是很庆幸，你们都没有受伤。要知道生命比一切都重要，有了生命才能去创造财富。不用担心，你还有我们这群朋友，我们会帮助你，支持你。只要我们团结一心，我们就能够度过这个难关的。希望你们也能重新振作。

祝好！

露西谨上

Dear Lucy,

Thank you for your letter. I am happy to have you to be my friend. Although I have lost a lot of things in the fire, it makes me know the importance of life and friendship. I believe that with your help, I will soon be able to rebuild my home. Thank you very much.

Best wishes!

Yours sincerely,

White

亲爱的露西：

很高兴收到你的来信，我很高兴有你们这样的朋友。虽然这次火灾让我失去了很多的东西，但教会了我生命和友谊的可贵。我相信有了你们的帮助，我很快就能重建我的家。衷心的谢谢你们。

祝好！

怀特谨上

Dear Lucy,

Your letter gives me a lot of comfort and courage. This disaster makes me scared. So during these days, I feel nervous, afraid and even desperate. I don't know how to continue my life. But I'm glad I'm not alone in this fight, because I have you, my best friends. I really don't know how to express my thanks. I hope we can be friends forever.

Best wishes!

Yours sincerely,

White

亲爱的露西：

你的来信给了我很大的安慰和勇气。这次的灾难让我非常害怕，所以这些日子以来我都很紧张和恐惧，更有绝望，不知道该怎么继续生活下去。但是我很高兴我并不是一个人在战斗，我有你们，我最珍贵的朋友。我真不知道该说什么表达我的感谢，但愿我们的友谊天长地久。

祝好！

怀特谨上

范本六 | 洪水慰问

Dear White,

The floods took many people's life and property as before. Your village was also attacked by the floods. I know you have suffered a lot. I hope you can face it bravely. Let's overcome this difficulty together. Let's struggle against the floods. I believe that we can quickly rebuild our homes.

Best wishes!

Yours sincerely,

Lucy

亲爱的怀特：

这次的洪水和往年一样，夺走了很多人的生命和财产。你的村子也遭受到了洪水的袭击，我知道你很痛苦。我希望你能勇敢面对，和我们一起战胜这个困难，让我们众志成城，与这场洪水做斗争。我相信我们能够很快地重建家园。

祝好！

露西谨上

Dear Lucy,

Thank you for writing to me at this moment. I really get much comfort. I'll look after myself and recover as soon as possible. Then we can rebuild our homes together.

Best wishes!

Yours sincerely,

White

亲爱的露西：

谢谢你能够在这个时候给我写信，我真的得到了很大的安慰。我会好好照顾自己，让自己能够尽快恢复，然后和大家一起重建我们的家园。

祝好！

怀特谨上

Dear Lucy,

What you said is right. This is not the time for me to be despair. More difficulties we are faced with, more quickly we should snap out of them. We shall not be knocked down by them. We should support each other and help each other. Thank you very much for your letter to comfort me and give me strength.

Best wishes!

Yours sincerely,

White

亲爱的露西：

你说的很对，现在不是绝望的时候。越到困难的时候，我们越要振作，这样才不会被困难打倒。我们应该相互扶持，相互帮助。非常感谢你能够写信安慰我，给我力量。

祝好！

怀特谨上

范本七 | 地震慰问

Dear White,

I am really sad to hear this news. And I'm sorry to hear that you have lost your mother in the earthquake. I hope you can get out of the shadow, and embrace the bright future. You have to know that there are a lot of things you should do. You are not alone. As your friends, we will always be at your side to support you. I hope you can be back to be optimistic as soon as possible. We all miss you.

Best wishes!

Yours sincerely,

Lucy

亲爱的怀特：

听到这个消息我真的很伤心，听到你在地震中失去了你的妈妈我很难过。我希望你能早日走出这个阴影，更好地走向未来。你要知道还有很多的事情等着你去完成，你并不孤单，我们这群朋友会一直在你的身边支持你，希望你能够尽快恢复成原来那个开朗的你。我们都很想你。

祝好！

露西谨上

Dear Lucy,

I am glad to receive your greetings. I feel much better now. I know your concern. Thank you very much.

Best wishes!

Yours sincerely,

White

亲爱的露西：

很高兴收到你的来信问候。我现在已经好多了，你们的心意我也都了解。谢谢你们。

祝好！

怀特谨上

Dear Lucy,

Although I know that I should cheer up, I feel it is really hard to accept the reality. The earthquake killed my dearest mother. I am very sad about this. I don't know what to do. It seems I suddenly lose everything, my family and my home. But thank you anyway. Your letter makes me feel much better. Don't worry. I think I'll recover soon, but I still need some time.

Best wishes!

Yours sincerely,

White

亲爱的露西：

虽然我知道我应该振作，但是我真的很难接受这个现实。这场地震夺走了我最爱的妈妈，我真的非常非常的伤心。我不知道该怎么做，我好像一下子失去了所有的东西，我的家人，我的家。但是很感谢你，看到你的来信我感觉好多了。你放心，我想我会很快恢复的，只是我还需要一些时间。

祝好！

怀特谨上

读书笔记

Lesson 11 吊唁信

如何写吊唁信

ⓐ 首先写明自己对收到的信息表示震惊、遗憾。

ⓑ 说明失去某人是对方的极大损失，安慰对方。赞扬逝世之人的品德与事迹。表达如果对方需要，自己愿意竭尽所能给予帮助。

ⓒ 给予对方最深切的慰问。

实用例句

1. I heard you had lost ... This is such a dreadful shock and I just want to tell you that I am so sorry to hear this news.

   我听说你失去了……这真是个可怕的消息。我只想告诉你听到这个消息我很难过。

2. I am sorry for your losing your love.

   我很难过你失去了你的爱人。

3. We will miss him forever.

   我们将会永远怀念他。

4. But the good memories will comfort you.

   但是回忆将会陪伴着你，安慰你。

5. If you need help, please let me know, and I will try my best...

   如果你需要帮助，请告诉我，我会竭尽所能……

6. The sudden passing of ...was a great shock to me.

   ……的突然过世让我很震惊。

7. I hope you can live on.

   我希望你可以继续好好活着。

8. With deep sympathy.

   送上我深深的同情。

9. Please accept my sincere condolence.

   请接受我真挚的吊唁。

10. You have my heartfelt sympathy.

    送上我发自内心的同情。

范本一 | 吊唁亲人

Dear Emily,

It is a dreadful shock to hear that your dad, my uncle, passed away yesterday. I am so sorry and so sad to hear this news.

He was a good man who always helped people around and gave me so much encouragement. I know how deeply you are affected. But he will always live in our memory. We will remember him forever.

Please call me if you want to talk to someone. I will always be here.

Yours sincerely,

Paula

亲爱的艾米丽：

听到昨天我叔叔，即你父亲，过世的消息，我感到非常震惊。听到这个消息我很难过。

他是一个很好的人，经常帮助身边的人，也给了我很多鼓励。我知道这件事对你影响很深，但是他会永远活在我们的记忆里，我们会永远想念着他。

如果你想找人聊聊的话请打电话给我，我会一直在你身边的。

宝拉谨上

Dear Paula,

Thank you for your letter. Thank you for comforting me.

It is hard to accept the fact that my father is dead. I can't believe that the person who is always staying with me has just gone. I feel really sad. I think I need some time to accept this fact. And I will recover from this a few days later.

Thank you for your concern.

Yours sincerely,

Emily

亲爱的宝拉：

谢谢你的来信。谢谢你能在我的身边支持我。

父亲去世这个事实我实在难以接受，我不敢相信一直陪在我身边的爸爸就这样走了。我真的非常伤心，我想我需要时间来接受这个事实。过段时间后，我想我会恢复的。

谢谢你的关心。

艾米丽谨上

Dear Paula,

Thank you for your concern. I'm glad that you are at my side to support me.

I am painful during this period. I know my dad really have left me forever. I will cheer up; I will go out from this shadow of sadness. I will be happy as my dad wished.

Thank you. Wish you healthy.

Yours sincerely,
Emily

亲爱的宝拉：

谢谢你的关心。我很庆幸还有你们在我身边。

这段日子对我来说真的很痛苦。我知道爸爸真的永远离开我了，我一定会振作，我会从悲伤中走出来，像爸爸希望的那样，快乐地活下去。

谢谢你。祝你健康。

艾米丽谨上

范本二 | 吊唁同事

Dear Emily,

I was shocked to hear John's death. A few days ago we had just discussed something about our work together, but now we can never meet again.

He is a very honest, brave, and smart man. Everyone loves him. We will miss him forever. He will always be my partner. As his wife, I hope you can live on for yourself, and take care of your children. As long as you need, we will always be there for you.

Please accept our sincere condolences.

Yours sincerely,
Paula

亲爱的艾米丽：

听到约翰去世的消息我很震惊。前几天我们还在一块儿商量工作的事情，现在却天人永隔了。

他是个非常正直、勇敢、聪明的人，深受大家喜爱。我们会永远怀念他的，他永远是我们的伙伴。作为他的妻子，希望你要好好地继续生活下去，照顾好你的孩子。只要你有需要，我们永远会在你身边支持你的。

请接受我们衷心的哀悼。

宝拉谨上

Dear Paula,

Thank you for your greetings. Thank you very much for giving me so much encouragement. I'll take care of my children. I'll miss him forever.

Thank you very much. Also bless you.

Yours sincerely,

Emily

亲爱的宝拉：

谢谢你的来信问候。非常感谢你能够给我这么大的鼓励，我会好好照顾我的孩子，我会永远怀念着他。

真的很感谢你，也祝福你。

艾米丽谨上

Dear Paula,

Your letter gives me great comfort. I'm glad my husband has such a good friend like you.

I know I still have a long way to go. I'll miss the days which my husband and I have spent together. I will raise my children up in a good environment, healthily and happily.

Thank you for your help and support. Wish you all the best!

Yours sincerely,

Emily

亲爱的宝拉：

你的来信给了我很大的安慰，我很高兴我丈夫能有你这样的朋友。

我知道以后还有很长的路要走。我会怀念我和他度过的美好时光，并抚养我们的孩子，让他们健康幸福地成长。

非常感谢你给予的帮助和支持。祝福你。

艾米丽谨上

范本三 | 吊唁同事亲属

Dear Emily,

I'm sorry to hear the news of your mother's death. You often mention your mother. I know she's a good, virtuous mother. She is the most important person in your heart. You must be very sad. I hope you can be strong enough to face this. I will always be here by your side to support you. If you need help, please tell me and I'll arrive at you as soon as possible.

  With deep sympathy.

Yours sincerely,
Paula

亲爱的艾米丽：

  听到你妈妈过世的消息我很难过。我常常听你提起你的母亲，我知道她是个善良，贤惠的好母亲。她是你最重要的人，你一定非常伤心。我希望你能够坚强地面对，我会在你身边永远支持你。如果你需要帮助，请告诉我，我会第一时间赶到你身边。

  表示深深的同情。

宝拉谨上

Dear Paula,

  I'm very gratified to receive your letter. You know me very well. My mother is the most important person to me. I will remember my mother's smile forever, be brave and strong to live on. I'll let Mom see my growth.

  Thanks for your concern.

Yours sincerely,
Emily

亲爱的宝拉：

  收到你的来信我很欣慰。你真的很了解我，妈妈在我心里是最重要的人。我会永远记得妈妈的笑，勇敢坚强地活下去。我会让妈妈看到我的成长。

  谢谢你的关心。

艾米丽谨上

Dear Paula,

  I'm lucky to have you be my friend. Your comfort and encouragement have given me courage. I will be strong enough to face this situation, so don't worry about me. I'll take care of myself.

  Thank you for your concern.

Yours sincerely,
Emily

亲爱的宝拉：

我很庆幸能有你这个朋友。你的安慰和鼓励给了我勇气，我会坚强地面对，不用太担心我，我会自己照顾自己。

谢谢你的关心。

艾米丽谨上

范本四｜吊唁领袖逝世

Dear Emily,

There are no words that can express our great sadness at losing your father's passing away. He was a very great mayor. Under his leadership, our living standards have greatly improved. Every aspect of life has a big development. We respect him very much. His death is a great loss to our city. We'll miss him forever, just like you.

If you need help, please tell me. We will be here to support you.

Please accept our sincere condolences.

Yours sincerely,
Paula

亲爱的艾米丽：

没有什么语言能够表达我们失去你父亲的伤痛。他是个非常了不起的市长，在他的带领下，我们的生活水平有了很大的提高，各个方面有了很大的发展。我们都非常尊敬他，失去他是我们市的极大损失，我们会像你一样永远怀念他。

如果需要帮助，请告诉我。我们大家都会在你身边的。

请接受我们真挚的吊唁。

宝拉谨上

Dear Paula,

Thank you for your condolences. I am so happy my father's efforts can get your recognition. I think he was glad to devote himself to make some contribution to our hometown. I will set him as an example and do whatever I can do to make contribution to the city.

Thank you for your concern.

Yours sincerely,
Emily

亲爱的宝拉：

　　谢谢你的吊唁，很高兴父亲的努力能够得到大家的认可。我觉得他非常高兴能为自己的家乡贡献自己的一份力量。我也会向父亲学习，尽我所能为这个城市贡献自己的一份力量。

　　谢谢你们的关心。

艾米丽谨上

Dear Paula,

　　Your letter gave me great comfort. Thank you very much for your affirmation to my father. He was always doing what he loved, and he was also proud of what he did. I am also very proud of him. His death was a shock to us, but what he did will be in our memories forever. We will miss him too. I will work together with you to have a new start.

　　Thank you for standing by my side to support me. Thank you very much.

Yours sincerely,

Emily

亲爱的宝拉：

　　你们的来信给了我很大的安慰，非常感谢你们能肯定我父亲。父亲他一直做着自己热爱的事业，为自己的事业自豪，我也很为他自豪。他的逝世对于我们来说都是个巨大的打击，但是他所做的一切都会留在我们的脑海里，我们会永远怀念他。我会和你们一起共同努力，重新出发。

　　非常感谢有你们陪在我的身边支持我。我真的非常感谢大家。

艾米丽谨上

范本五｜讣文

Obituary

　　×××has passed away in×××Hospital on 12th September, 2011 at the age of 83. His farewell ceremony will be held in the×××Church at 2 pm tomorrow.

×××

9.13

讣告

　　×××于2011年9月12号在×××医院去世，享年83岁。他的告别仪式将在明天下午两点于×××教堂举行。

×××

9.13

Obituary

Because of the incurable cancer, × × × has passed away in the × × × Hospital at 10: 23 am on May 13th, 2012 at the age of 88. As he wished, there is no farewell ceremony held.

× × ×

5.14

讣告

由于癌症医治无效，× × ×于2012年5月13日早晨10: 23在× × ×医院去世，享年88岁。遵照他的遗嘱，不举行遗体告别仪式。

× × ×

5.14

读书笔记

Lesson 12　感谢信

如何写感谢信

ⓐ首先表达对对方的庆贺、慰问、款待和帮忙的感谢。

ⓑ表达自己的感想，赞扬对方，语气要真诚。

ⓒ送上祝福和感谢。

实用例句

1. Thank you for your concern about my baby.

   谢谢你对我孩子的关心。

2. It is kind of you to send me a birthday present.

   谢谢你送我生日礼物。

3. I really appreciate your wishes.

   我真的很感谢你的祝福。

4. It is good to hear from you to give me such important advice.

   能够收到你的来信我很高兴，谢谢你给我这个很好的建议。

5. Please accept my thanks not only for the letter but also for the good wishes.

   请接受我的谢意，不仅是因为你的来信，也为你的祝福。

6. I am so happy to have a friend like you who always give me so much help and support.

   我很高兴能有你这样的朋友，经常给我很多帮助和支持。

7. Your letter gives me so much comfort and happiness and reminds me that I have such a good friend.

   你的来信给了我很大的安慰和快乐，提醒我有这样一个知心的朋友在我身边。

8. Thank you once again.

   再次表示感谢。

9. I know you can always get what I think and what I would like to do. It's my luck to have you to be my side.

   我知道你总是能够猜到我心里所想，所要做的，有你在我的身边是我的幸运。

10. With my best wishes to you!

    祝你一切都好！

范本一 | 感谢招待

Dear Alice,

Thank you very much for inviting me to your house for dinner last night, and I feel so happy to have dinner with you and your family.

I am also very happy to see your family. They are very kind. The food cooked by your mom were really delicious. This will be one of my best memories in my life. Hope you will have time to come to my house to have dinner with my family. I also want to introduce my family members to you.

Thank you for your warm hospitality.

Yours sincerely,

Anna

亲爱的爱丽丝:

非常谢谢你昨晚邀请我去你家吃饭,能与你和你的家人一起吃饭真的很愉快。

很高兴能够见到你的家人,他们都非常热情。你妈妈烧的菜非常好吃。这将是我一段最美好的记忆。也希望你有时间可以来我家一起吃个晚饭,我也想把我的家人介绍给你。

谢谢你们的热情招待。

安娜谨上

Dear Anna,

I'm glad you enjoy the dinner. And thank you very much for your invitation. I'm happy to go to your house to have dinner with your family.

Best wishes!

Yours sincerely,

Alice

亲爱的安娜:

我很高兴你喜欢这次的聚餐,也非常感谢你的邀请。我非常高兴去你家和你家人共进晚餐。

祝好!

爱丽丝谨上

Dear Anna,

I am glad to receive your letter. My mom is happy to hear that you like the dishes. Hope you can come to my house once again. I also thank you very much for your invitation. And I would feel honored to have dinner with your family.

Best wishes!

Yours sincerely,

Alice

亲爱的安娜：

很高兴收到你的回信。我妈妈听说你喜欢她做的菜，她很高兴。希望下次还可以来我家玩。我也非常谢谢你的邀请，能和你的家人一起共进晚餐是我的荣幸。

祝好！

爱丽丝谨上

范本二 | 感谢来信

Dear Alice,

I'm very pleased to receive your letter asking me about my condition. Your letter gives me a lot of comfort; it reminds me of you as a good friend in my side.

Recently I have a lot of things to do, like moving to a new house and doing the housework, so I had no enough time to have a rest, and I was sick. But the doctor said it was nothing, and I just needed to have a good rest, and had something full of nutrition. Now I feel better, especially after receiving your letter. I hope you can take care of your body, and keep a happy mood.

Thank you for your concern. Wish you all the best.

Yours sincerely,

Anna

亲爱的爱丽丝：

我很高兴收到你的来信询问我的病情。你的来信给了我很大的安慰，它提醒我有你这样一个好朋友在我身边。

最近由于事情比较多，又要忙着搬家，又要做家务，没有足够的休息时间，所以就病倒了。但是医生说没什么大的问题，只是需要多休息，补充营养。现在我已经感觉好多了，尤其是收到你的来信后。希望你也要注意身体，保持心情愉快。

谢谢你的关心。祝一切顺利。

安娜谨上

Dear Anna,

You are my best friend, and I just did what a friend should do. I am glad to know my letter gives you so much encouragement. I hope you can recover soon.

Best wishes!

Yours sincerely,

Alice

亲爱的安娜：

你是我最重要的朋友，关心你是我应该做的事情。很高兴我的信能给你这么大的鼓励，希望你早日恢复健康。

祝好！

爱丽丝谨上

Dear Anna,

I just did what a friend should do. And if you need help, please let me know. I will try my best to help you. I hope you can take care of yourself and don't be too tired.

Best wishes!

Yours sincerely,

Alice

亲爱的安娜：

我只是做了一个朋友应该做的。如果你需要帮助，请记得联系我，我一定会尽我所能帮助你。希望你好好保重自己，不要过于劳累。

祝好！

爱丽丝谨上

范本三 | 感谢来访

Dear Alice,

Thank you to come to my house, with so many gifts for my family. We all like your gifts. You are so sweet. It's a pleasure that we can have dinner together. Thank you very much for your praise of my house.

Your visit to my house really made us very happy.

Best wishes!

Yours sincerely,

Anna

亲爱的爱丽丝：

很感谢你能来我家，还带了这么多礼物送给我的家人。我们都非常喜欢你的礼物，你真贴心，能和你一起共进晚餐真是件令人愉快的事情。非常感谢你对我家的赞美。

你能来我家真是令我们很高兴。

祝好！

安娜谨上

Dear Anna,

I'm very glad to visit you. I like the decoration of your house and your garden. I also love the dishes that your mother cooked for me. They were so delicious that I can't forget them. It is so happy to have dinner and chat with you and your family.

Wish you all the best!

Yours sincerely,

Alice

亲爱的安娜：

我很高兴能去你家进行参观。我很喜欢你家的装饰，还有你家的花园，也非常喜欢你妈妈为我烧的菜，让我很难忘。能和你的家人一起吃饭、聊天真是一件愉快的事。

祝你一切都好！

爱丽丝谨上

Dear Anna,

I am happy to go to your house to have a visit. I think I know much better of you after visiting your home. I envy you that your parents and your brother love you so much. I felt very nice in your home. I hope I can have another chance to visit.

Best wishes!

Yours sincerely,

Alice

亲爱的安娜：

我很高兴能够去你家玩。我觉得到过你家之后我对你有了更深的了解，知道你有那么疼爱你的爸妈，还有哥哥，我很羡慕。你们家很热闹，很温馨。希望下次还有机会可以去玩。

祝好！

爱丽丝谨上

范本四 | 感谢帮助

Dear Alice,

Thank you for helping me find so much information I need. I also have a lot of things to do. Taking you so much time, I feel so sorry to ask you to help me find the materials that I was badly in need of. I feel lucky to have a friend like you who can give me help in time to solve my problems. You are really a warm-hearted and kind person. Thanks to your materials, I can finish my report very well.

Thank you very much!

Yours sincerely,

Anna

亲爱的爱丽丝：

非常感谢你帮我找了那么多我需要的资料。我知道你也有很多事情要做，让你花时间帮我找资料实在不好意思。很庆幸有你这样一个朋友，在我有困难的时候能够及时帮我解决问题。你真是一个热心、善良的人。多亏了你的资料，我才能更好得完成我的报告。

非常感谢你！

安娜谨上

Dear Anna,

I am so glad that these materials can help you finish your report. We are friends and we are supposed to help each other. I think if I need your help, you will also help me immediately.

Best wishes!

Yours sincerely,

Alice

亲爱的安娜：

　　这些资料能够对你有所帮助我很高兴。我们是朋友，互相帮助是应该的。我想要是我有事情需要你的帮助，你也会立刻帮助我的。

　　祝好！

爱丽丝谨上

Dear Anna,

　　Thank you for giving me so much praise. I am also very happy that I can help you. These materials had already been prepared, and it didn't take me so much time to collect them. So you don't need to feel sorry. I'm glad you can think of me when you have difficulties. And I also feel lucky to have a friend like you.

　　I wish you all the best!

Yours sincerely,

Alice

亲爱的安娜：

　　谢谢你能够这么肯定我，我也很高兴自己能够帮到你。这些资料我刚好有，并没有花费我多少时间，所以不要感到抱歉。我很高兴你有困难的时候能够想到我，我也很高兴有你这样一个朋友。

　　祝你一切顺利！

爱丽丝谨上

范本五 | 感谢咨询

Dear Alice,

　　Thank you very much to consult relevant new products of my company. The new phone of our company has a lot of functions, including photography, internet access, video chat and so on. I have made a detailed explanation to you when you consulted it to me. I'm very glad you pay so much attention to our company and the products. This will make us more confident and create better new products to satisfy customers.

　　I hope you can continue to pay attention to our products, and also welcome you to come again for consultation. We will give you a satisfactory reply.

　　Best wishes!

Yours sincerely,

Anna

亲爱的爱丽丝：

非常感谢你向我们公司咨询有关新产品。我们公司新出的这款手机具有很多功能，包括照相、上网、视频聊天等功能，在你咨询的时候我给你做过很详细的解释。我非常高兴你能关注我们公司以及公司的产品，这让我们更有信心创造新的产品满足顾客的需求。

希望你能继续关注我们的产品，也欢迎你再来咨询，我们一定会给你满意的答复。

祝好！

安娜谨上

Dear Anna,

Thank you for your introduction. I'm glad I can get useful information by consulting you. I like your products very much. And I always concern about your new products. I hope you can continue to work hard, and create more and better products. I will support you.

Best wishes!

Yours sincerely,
Alice

亲爱的安娜：

谢谢你的介绍，我很高兴通过咨询你能够获得有用的信息。你们的产品我一直以来都很喜欢，也很关注你们新产品的推出。我希望你们能够继续努力，创造更多更好的产品。我会支持你们的。

祝好！

爱丽丝谨上

Dear Anna,

I'm very pleased to receive your letter. Thank you for your detailed introduction, so I can know much about the new phone which your company will launch. I also wish that your company will be better. I'm looking forward to your new mobile phones.

Best wishes!

Yours sincerely,
Alice

亲爱的安娜：

我很高兴收到你的来信。谢谢你的详细介绍，让我对你们公司即将推出的新款手机有更好的了解，也希望你们的公司会越做越好。我很期待这个新款手机。

祝好！

爱丽丝谨上

范本六 | 感谢邀请

Dear Alice,

It is so nice of you to invite me to your party. I am very glad to come. I know it is a big party to celebrate your parents' 20th wedding anniversary. I am so happy to hear this. And I hope we can have a good night in your house. Thank you for inviting me and send my best wishes to your parents.

Wish you all the best!

Yours sincerely,
Anna

亲爱的爱丽丝：

谢谢你能邀请我参加你们家的派对，我非常愿意前往。我知道这是你父母结婚二十周年纪念的大派对，我听到这个消息真高兴，我希望能在你家度过美好的一晚。谢谢你邀请我，请送上我对你父母真挚的问候。

祝你一切顺利！

安娜谨上

Dear Anna,

We all appreciate that you will come to the party. Thank you for being my guest. And I hope you can enjoy yourself that night.

Best wishes!

Yours sincerely,
Alice

亲爱的安娜：

很感谢你能出席我们的派对，感谢你来我家做客，希望那天你能玩的开心。

祝好！

爱丽丝谨上

Dear Anna,

I want you know that I am so happy that you can come to the party. I want to share this moment with all my friends. And I wish we can have a good time that night. And thank you for your best wishes to my parents. It is so thoughtful of you. Thank you very much.

Best wishes!

Yours sincerely,

Alice

亲爱的安娜：

我想让你知道我很高兴你能来参加这个派对。我想要和我所有的朋友分享这个欢乐的时刻，我希望我们都能玩得开心。非常感谢你对我爸妈的祝福，谢谢你如此体贴。

祝好！

爱丽丝谨上

范本七 | 感谢合作

Dear Alice,

Our project is finally finished. Thanks to you, we can finish it so quickly. I'm glad to have you to be my partner. You're very good, and there are a lot of people who want to ask you to be their partner, but finally you chose me. In this process, you gave me a lot of help and care. Because of you, this project can be finished so smoothly.

Thank you for your contribution to this cooperation. I hope there will be more opportunities to cooperate. Thank you very much.

I wish you all the best!

Yours sincerely,

Anna

亲爱的爱丽丝：

我们的项目终于完成了。这多亏了你我们才能这么快完成，我真庆幸能有你这个合作伙伴。你很优秀，有很多人都想要找你当他们的合作伙伴，但是最后你却选择了我。在这个过程中，你给了我很大的帮助和关心。因为有你，才能使得这个项目这么顺利地完成。

我非常感谢你能够促成这次的合作，希望以后有更多的机会合作。非常感谢。

祝你一切顺利！

安娜谨上

Dear Anna,

I am very happy to receive your letter, and thank you for your praise. I think you are a very excellent person who is worthy to cooperate with. In this project, I learned a lot from you. I also hope we can have another opportunity to cooperate again.

Best wishes!

Yours sincerely,

Alice

亲爱的安娜：

收到你的来信我很高兴，谢谢你对我的赞美。我觉得你是一个非常值得合作的人，你也是一个非常优秀的合作伙伴。这次的项目，我在你身上学到很多。我也希望能有机会再次合作。

祝好！

爱丽丝谨上

Dear Anna,

Thank you for saying so. But I think it is the result of our common efforts. I think we should celebrate the achievement of this project, so I propose a celebration party to comfort ourselves. And you can make the time and the place.

Best wishes !

Yours sincerely,

Alice

亲爱的安娜：

谢谢你这样说，但是我认为这是我们共同努力的结果。我觉得我们应该庆祝一下这个项目的完成，所以我提议举行一个庆功派对来犒劳一下自己，时间和地点由你来定。

祝好！

爱丽丝谨上

范本八 | 感谢赠送礼品

Dear Alice,

I want to thank you for the flowers you gave me. You know recently I have been upset about life and work. But when I look at them, I feel very comfortable and happy. They remind me that I have such a good friend like you who always help me come out of the frustration. They cheer me up and give me the power. Thank you very much, my dear friend.

Best wishes!

Yours sincerely,

Anna

亲爱的爱丽丝：

我想要谢谢你送我花。你知道最近我对生活和工作都很沮丧，但是每当我看着它们的时候，总是能让我感到舒服和开心。它们提醒着我，我有你这样的朋友在我身边，经常帮助我走出沮丧。它们让我的心情能够放松，给我力量。真的非常感谢你，我亲爱的朋友。

祝好！

安娜谨上

Dear Anna,

I'm glad my flowers could give you so much comfort. I know recently your mood is not very good, and you also had a lot of things to do. I want to do something for you. I think these flowers will make you feel my concern.

Wish you all good!

Yours sincerely,

Alice

亲爱的安娜：

我很高兴我的花能给你这么大的安慰。我知道最近你的心情不是很好，又有很多事情要做，我很想为你做点什么。我想这些花能够让你感受到我的关心。

希望你一切都好！

爱丽丝谨上

Dear Anna,

Do you know that a friend is the person who will give you help and support when you're sad? I am really happy that the flowers I sent to you can give you so much comfort. I want you to know that I will always be in your side to support you. So if you have anything to say or anything to do, please tell me, and I will accompany you forever.

Best wishes!

Yours sincerely,

Alice

亲爱的安娜：

你知道吗？朋友就是在你难过的时候给你帮助和支持的人。我真的很高兴，我送你的花给你这么多安慰。我要你知道你一直有我陪在你的身边支持你。所以有任何想说的话，想要做的事，请告诉我，我会陪你一起。

祝好！

爱丽丝谨上

范本九 | 感谢师长教诲

Dear teacher,

I am very happy to become one of your students. During this period, you have cared so much about my life and study.

You always give me a lot of encouragement in my life. You give me so much patience in my study, and teach me how to think and how to do right. When I was writing my paper, you spent a lot of time helping me rewrite my article, and pointing the problems for me. When I graduated from school, you gave me so many suggestions and opinions. I'm really very grateful to your help. You are like a friend who gives me a lot of support and help. I'm glad you can be my teacher.

I wish you healthy and live a happy life.

Yours sincerely,

Anna

亲爱的老师：

能够成为您的学生我很高兴。在这段时期，您总是非常关心我的生活和学习。

在生活上，您总是给予我很多鼓励。在学习上您总是能够耐心地教导我，引导我做正确的思考。在我写论文的时候，您花了大量的时间帮我改写我的文章，帮我指出问题。在毕业时候，给予我很多意见和建议。真的非常感谢老师您的帮助，您就像朋友一样这么支持我，帮助我，我很庆幸能够有您这样一位老师。

祝你身体健康，生活愉快。

安娜谨上

Dear Anna,

I am happy to receive your letter. As a teacher, the happiest thing for me is to see the growth of my students. You are just like my children, and I am so happy to company you to have the wonderful life in the college. I hope you can work hard and get great achievement.

Best wishes!

Yours sincerely,
Alice

亲爱的安娜：

收到你的来信我很高兴。作为一名老师，最开心的就是看到自己的学生有所成长。你们都像我的孩子一样，我很高兴能够伴随着你们度过最美好的大学生活。希望你以后能够努力工作，获得更大的进步。

祝好！

爱丽丝谨上

Dear Anna,

I am so proud to have you be my student. You are the most talented student that I have ever taught. You can always come up with good ideas. And you are also a strong girl in your life. Seeing your progress, I am very pleased. I also learnt a lot from you.

I hope you can continue to work hard, and I think you will have a better future.

Best wishes!

Yours sincerely,
Alice

亲爱的安娜：

　　我很骄傲有你这样的学生，你是我教过的最有才华的学生。你总是能够有很好的想法，生活中你也是个坚强的孩子。看到你不断进步，我非常欣慰，我也从你身上学到很多东西。

　　希望你继续努力，有个更好的未来。

　　祝好！

爱丽丝谨上

读书笔记

Lesson 13 邀请信

如何写邀请信

ⓐ 直接说明为何邀请对方，并希望对方能来。

ⓑ 写明活动的时间、地点等要素，能够让对方事先安排时间。

ⓒ 衷心地希望对方能够来参加，表达自己的感谢和祝福。

实用例句

1. I am writing to invite you to come for a luncheon with my family. And I hope you can come.

   我写信是想邀请你参加我们家的午宴，我希望你能来。

2. Will you have a dinner with me and my wife to celebrate the success of the project?

   你能来我家和我与我的妻子一起吃个晚饭，庆祝这个项目的成功吗？

3. Bob and I will give a party and we wish you can come to have fun with us. It will start at 18：00 on Sunday night. Looking forward to seeing you!

   我和鲍勃将会举行一个派对，我们希望你能来玩。聚会将在周日晚上18：00开始，期待见到你。

4. If it is convenient for you, would you like to join in the party we will hold on Saturday night at 18：00? I really hope you can come.

   如果方便的话，你能来参加我们周六晚上18：00举行的派对吗？我真的非常希望你能来。

5. Tomorrow is my birthday and I want to ask you to come to my house to have the party. It will start at 9：00 a.m. on Sunday.

   明天是我的生日，我想邀请你来我家参加我的生日派对，派对将会在周日早上9：00开始。

6. I will be happy if you can come to my house to have dinner next Thursday at 16：00.

   如果你能在下周四16：00来我家和我一起吃晚饭我会很高兴的。

7. I think it will be great fun to see the wonderful movie together. Would you

like to come with me?

我觉得我们一起去看一部电影将会很开心，你愿意来吗？

8. This Sunday I will have a wedding banquet in the ×××hotel at 17：00. It would give me so much pleasure if you can come to join us and share the happiness with us.

这个周日17：00我将会在×××酒店举行婚宴。如果你能来参加，和我一起分享我的喜悦，我会很高兴的。

9. Thank you for your concern. I am looking forward to seeing you in the party.

谢谢你的关心，我很期待能在聚会上看到你。

10. It's my honor if you can come to join us and best wishes!

如果你能来将是我的荣幸，祝福你。

范本一 | 邀请参加婚宴

Dear Ming,

　　I am happy to tell you that on Sunday I will have a wedding banquet in the ××× hotel at 17：00. It would give me so much pleasure if you can come to join us and share the happiness with us. I am looking forward to seeing you at the banquet.

　　Best wishes!

Yours sincerely,
Hua

亲爱的明：

　　我很高兴告诉你这周日17：00我将会在×××酒店举行婚宴，如果你能来参加，和我一起分享我的喜悦，我会很高兴的。我很期待能在宴会上见到你。

　　祝好!

华谨上

Dear Hua,

　　I am so happy to hear this news. And it is so nice of you to invite me to your wedding banquet. And I will arrive there on time. Congratulations!

　　Wish you all the best!

Yours sincerely,
Ming

亲爱的华：

　　我真的很高兴听到这个消息，非常感谢你能够邀请我参加你的婚宴，我会准时到达的。祝贺你！

　　祝你一切顺利！

　　　　　　　　　　　　　　　　　　　　　　　　　　　　　明谨上

Dear Hua,

I am so pleased to know this wonderful news from your letter. I am so happy for you. Congratulations on your marriage. But I am so sorry to tell you that I can't go to the banquet that day, because I have to go abroad for a lecture. I am so sorry. Thank you for your invitation.

Wish you all the best.

　　　　　　　　　　　　　　　　　　　　　　　　　　　Yours sincerely,

　　　　　　　　　　　　　　　　　　　　　　　　　　　　　Ming

亲爱的华：

　　我很高兴收到你的来信告知我这个好消息。我很为你高兴，祝贺你结婚，但是我很抱歉不能参加你的婚礼，因为我那天要出国做个报告，我很遗憾。谢谢你的邀请。

　　祝你一切顺利！

　　　　　　　　　　　　　　　　　　　　　　　　　　　　　明谨上

范本二 | 邀请出席会议

Dear Mr. Zhang,

Next Sunday we will have a meeting in ××× University about the education of the college students. And it is our honor to invite you to attend this meeting to discuss this issue with all the professors. We are looking forward to your coming.

Best wishes!

　　　　　　　　　　　　　　　　　　　　　　　　　　　Yours sincerely,

　　　　　　　　　　　　　　　　　　　　　　　　　　　　　Li Hua

亲爱的张先生：

　　下周日我们将会在×××大学举行一个关于大学生教育的会议，如果您能来参加这个会议与所有的教授一起讨论这个话题将会是我们的荣幸。我们期待您的光临。

祝好！

李华谨上

Dear Mr. Li,

Thank you for asking me to come to the meeting. I think the education of college students is not only important to the students but also meaningful to our country. So it is necessary for us to discuss this topic. I really would like to come.

Best wishes!

Yours sincerely,

Zhang Ming

亲爱的李先生：

谢谢你邀请我参加这个会议。我认为大学教育无论是对大学生本身还是对我们国家来说都是非常重要的，所以讨论这个话题是非常有必要的，我真的很乐意参加。

祝好！

张明谨上

Dear Mr. Li,

Thank you for asking me to attend this meeting, but I am so sorry to tell you that I have another meeting on that day. I have promised them a few days ago, so I can't attend your meeting. I am so sorry.

Best wishes!

Yours sincerely,

Zhang Ming

亲爱的李先生：

谢谢你邀请我参加这个会议，但是很抱歉，我在那天有另外一个会议要参加。这个会议我几天前就已经答应了，所以我就不能去参加你们的会议。非常抱歉。

祝好！

张明谨上

范本三 | 邀请参加庆典

Dear Mr. Zhang，

On September 24th, our school will have the 50th anniversary celebration. And I would like to invite you to come to join us. The celebration will begin at 9: 30 am on the square of the school. Wish to see you here.

Best wishes!

Yours sincerely,

Li Hua

亲爱的张先生：

9月24号，我们学校将会举行建校五十周年的庆典活动，我想邀请您来参加。庆典将会在早上9：30在学校广场正式开始，我们期待您的光临。

祝好！

李华谨上

Dear Mr. Li，

Thank you for asking me to the celebration. I am glad to receive this invitation. And I really want to go to have a good time with my old friends in our alma mater. I will be there on time.

Best wishes!

Yours sincerely,

Zhang Ming

亲爱的李先生：

谢谢你邀请我参加这个庆典。我很高兴收到这个邀请信，我真的很想和我的老朋友们一起为母校庆祝，我会准时到的。

祝好！

张明谨上

Dear Mr. Li，

I am happy to hear this. Please allow me to send my heartiest wishes to my alma mater. However I am sorry that I have to miss this celebration that day, because I have to go on a business trip on that day. It is a pity to miss this.

Best wishes!

Yours sincerely,

Zhang Ming

亲爱的李先生：

　　我很高兴听到这个消息。请允许我为我的母校送上我最真心的祝福，但是很遗憾我不能参加这个庆典，因为我那天要出差。真的很遗憾。

　　祝好！

张明谨上

范本四 | 邀请参加生日派对

Dear Ming,

　　Tomorrow is my birthday and I want to invite you to come to my birthday party. It will start at 9: 00 am. It will be great fun to celebrate the birthday with my friends. And I wish you can come, and your coming will give me so much pleasure.

　　Best wishes!

Yours sincerely,

Hua

亲爱的明：

　　明天是我的生日，我想邀请你来我家参加我的生日派对，派对将会在早上9: 00开始。能和朋友们一起过生日会很有趣，我希望你能来，那样我会很高兴的。

　　祝好！

华谨上

Dear Hua,

　　I am so happy to hear the news and happy birthday to you! I would love to come. I will be there on time with my secret present. Wish to see you soon.

　　Best wishes!

Yours sincerely,

Ming

亲爱的华：

　　我很高兴听到这个消息，祝你生日快乐！我非常愿意参加，我会带着我的神秘小礼物准时到的。期待赶快见到你！

　　祝好！

明谨上

Dear Hua,

Thank you for inviting me to your birthday party and happy birthday to you! But I think I have no time to go to your house, because I have to go to Xinjiang with my supervisor to do an investigation. I am so sorry to tell you this.

Wish you have a happy birthday!

Yours sincerely,
Ming

亲爱的华：

谢谢你邀请我去参加你的生日派对，祝你生日快乐！但是我想我没有时间去你家了，因为我要和我的导师一起去新疆做一个调研。我很遗憾。

祝你过个愉快的生日！

明谨上

✉ 范本五 | 邀请外国来宾出席活动

Dear Mr. Brown,

I would like to invite you to attend my photography show about "life". I hope you can come and give me some comments and opinions on my photos. It will start at 10:00 am on August 11th. And the show will be held in the exhibition center on the Central Avenue.

Best wishes!

Yours sincerely,
Li Hua

亲爱的布朗先生：

我想邀请您参加我的主题为"生命"的摄影展。我希望您能来，也希望能够听到您对我的照片的一些评价和建议。活动会在8月11日上午10点开始，地点是市中心路的展览中心。

祝好！

李华谨上

Dear Hua,

Thank you for your invitation. I would like to come. I think you are a good photographer. I like your photos. And I am happy to hear that you will have a photography show. I will be there on time. Hope to see you soon.

Best wishes!

Yours sincerely,

Brown

亲爱的华：

　　谢谢你邀请我参加你的展览，我很愿意前往。我认为你是一个出色的摄影师，我喜欢你拍的照片，我很高兴听到你举行摄影展，我会准时到的。期待赶紧见到你！

　　祝好！

布朗谨上

Dear Hua,

I am so glad to hear from you. I am happy for you that you will have your own photography show. I hope I can come but I am so sorry to tell you that I have to miss it, because I have to go back to America for some days. So I can't go to your show.

Best wishes!

Yours sincerely,

Brown

亲爱的华：

　　我很高兴收到你的来信，我为你能够有自己的摄影展感到高兴。我希望我能去，但是很抱歉我去不了了，因为我要回美国几天。很抱歉错过你的展出。

　　祝好！

布朗谨上

读书笔记

Lesson 14 回复邀请信

如何写回复邀请信

ⓐ 首先对对方的邀请表示感谢，直接说明自己是否能去。

ⓑ 如果能去，说明到达的时间，表示自己非常期待；如果不能去，要说明理由，真诚地道歉。

ⓒ 表示感谢或表示抱歉，最后表达自己的祝福。

实用例句

1. Thank you very much to invite me to your wedding party. I would like to come and share the happiness with you.

非常感谢你邀请我参加你们的结婚派对。我很愿意参加，并与你们分享这美好的时刻。

2. I am so happy to hear the news that you are going to have a birthday party. And thank you for inviting me to your party.

我很高兴听到你要举行生日派对，谢谢你邀请我参加。

3. It is so nice of you to ask me to your home to have dinner with your family. I am eager to meet your family members.

谢谢你能邀请我去你家吃饭，我很期待能够与你家人见面。

4. I am so sorry to tell you that I have a meeting that day and have no time to participate in the party. It is a pity to miss this party and I hope you can enjoy yourselves.

我很抱歉那天我有个会议要参加，所以没有时间参加你的派对。错过这个派对真是遗憾，我希望你们玩得开心。

5. Unfortunately I have a rather important date that day. Please accept my sincere apology to miss your invitation.

不巧的是，那天我刚好有个很重要的约会。错过你的邀请，请接受我真诚的道歉。

6. I would love to come, but I have to leave the town to go on a business trip. I am sorry to tell you that.

我非常想去，但是我将要在那天离开市里去外地出差，我很抱歉告诉你这个消息。

7. It is so kind of you to ask me to go to the dinner but I am afraid that I am not able to come. I hope to have dinner with you next time.

谢谢你能邀请我共进晚餐，但是恐怕我不能够前往。我希望下次可以有机会和你一起吃饭。

8. I think that must be very exciting and I am eager to go.

我想那一定非常有趣，我很期待前往。

9. See you that day, so we can have a chat and enjoy a good time.

那天再见，到时候我们可以聊聊天，好好玩玩。

10. Thank you very much and I will arrive there on time.

谢谢你的邀请，我会准时到那里的。

范本一 | 接受邀请

Dear Henry,

I am so happy to receive your invitation of having dinner together with your family. I am looking forward to having dinner with you. We will arrive there about 5:30 pm. Thank you for your invitation. Hope we can have a nice day with you.

Best wishes!

Yours sincerely,

Betty

亲爱的亨利：

我很高兴收到你的晚宴邀请。我很期待能和你们共进晚餐，我们将会在那天下午5：30到你家，非常感谢你们的邀请，希望我们可以度过愉快的一晚。

祝好！

贝蒂谨上

Dear Betty,

Thank you for coming to our house to have dinner with me. I am eager to see you.

Best wishes!

Yours sincerely,

Henry

亲爱的贝蒂：

感谢你能来我家共进晚餐，我很期待见到你。

祝好！

亨利谨上

Dear Betty,

I am glad to hear that you can come to have dinner with me. We will start at 6: 00 pm, so take your time. I am looking forward to seeing you.

Beat wishes!

Yours sincerely,

Henry

亲爱的贝蒂：

我很高兴听到你能来参加我们晚宴的消息。我们会在下午六点开始，你不用着急。期待与你见面。

祝好！

亨利谨上

范本二 | 拒绝邀请

Dear Henry,

It is so nice of you to invite me to your birthday party. Happy birthday! I would love to come, but I have an important meeting that day. So I will miss the party. It is a pity for me. Please accept my best wishes to you. I hope you can enjoy your party and have a good time.

Best wishes!

Yours sincerely,

Betty

亲爱的亨利：

非常感谢你能邀请我参加你的生日派对，生日快乐！我非常愿意去，但是我在那天刚好有个很重要的会议，所以我将要错过这个派对了。这真是很遗憾，请接受我的祝福，希望你们玩得开心。

祝好！

贝蒂谨上

Dear Betty,

I feel so sorry to hear that you can't come to my party. But I can understand this. I think maybe next time we can celebrate on our own. I am looking forward to that.

Best wishes!

Yours sincerely,

Henry

亲爱的贝蒂：

听到你不能来的消息，我很遗憾，但是我能理解。我想也许下次我们可以单独庆祝，我很期待。

祝好！

亨利谨上

Dear Betty,

It is a pity that you can't come to my birthday party. You are my best friend. I really hope you can come. Maybe I can delay the party to wait for you to come. Please tell me when you have the time. I will wait for you.

Best wishes!

Yours sincerely,

Henry

亲爱的贝蒂：

你不能来真的很遗憾。你是我最好的朋友，我真的希望你能来。也许我可以延迟派对开始的时间等你来，请告诉我你的时间，我会等你。

祝好！

亨利谨上

范本三 | 回复邀请信（1）

Dear Henry,

I accept this invitation with great pleasure. I hope to have a cup of tea with you and chat with you about life and work. I will be there at 9:00 am on Monday. I am looking forward to seeing you.

Best wishes!

Yours sincerely,

Betty

亲爱的亨利：

　　我很高兴接受你的邀请。我希望能和你一起喝杯茶，聊聊生活和工作。我将会在周一早上九点到那里，很期待见到你。

　　祝好！

贝蒂谨上

Dear Betty,

　　I am so happy to hear that you can come. I think we will have a nice time together.

　　Best wishes!

Yours sincerely,
Henry

亲爱的贝蒂：

　　我很高兴听到你能来。我想我们一起会度过很美好的一天。

　　祝好！

亨利谨上

Dear Betty,

　　I am pleased that you accept my invitation to have tea together. Let's make the time at 9: 00 am on Monday. If you have any proposal, please let me know, so we can make a good schedule and have a nice day.

　　Best wishes!

Yours sincerely,
Henry

亲爱的贝蒂：

　　很高兴你能接受我的邀请一起喝茶，我们见面的时间就定在星期一早上的9: 00。如果你有别的提议就告诉我，我们可以制订一个很好的行程，这样我们将会度过美好而充实的一天。

　　祝好！

亨利谨上

范本四 | 回复邀请信（2）

Dear Henry,

　　I think it is a good idea to have a picnic together near the lake on Sunday morning at 9: 00. Thank you for asking me. As you suggested, I will arrive there at 8: 50 am to prepare. I am looking forward to seeing you.

Best wishes!

Yours sincerely,

Betty

亲爱的亨利：

周日早上九点在湖边野餐真是个很好的主意，很感谢你邀请我。如你建议的，我将在8：50到达那里准备准备。非常期待见到你。

祝好！

贝蒂谨上

Dear Betty,

I am glad to hear that you can come. I should remind you that you can take something to eat and drink. And I will take something to play. So we can play some games when we finish eating.

Best wishes!

Yours sincerely,

Henry

亲爱的贝蒂：

我很高兴你能来。我要提醒你一下，记得带上一点吃的和喝的，我会带上一些玩的东西，这样我们吃完就可以玩些游戏。

祝好！

亨利谨上

Dear Betty,

I think it is thoughtful of you to come there a little earlier for the preparation. And I hope we can have a good time there.

Best wishes!

Yours sincerely,

Henry

亲爱的贝蒂：

你决定早点到那里做些准备工作，我认为你想得真周到。希望我们可以度过美好的一天。

祝好！

亨利谨上

范本五 | 回复邀请信（3）

Dear Henry,

　　I am indeed sorry to say that I can't accept your invitation to come to your home to have dinner with you and your family, because I promised my grandmother to visit her and help to do some housework. So I could not go to your house to have dinner. I am sorry to let you down. Please accept my apology. I hope we can have dinner next time.

　　Thank you for your invitation again. Wish you have a good weekend.

Yours sincerely,

Betty

亲爱的亨利：

　　实在很抱歉，我不能接受你的邀请，去你家和你的家人一起吃晚饭。因为我已经答应我外婆要去她家帮她干家务，所以我不能去你家吃晚饭了。我很抱歉让你失望了，请接受我的道歉。我希望下次有机会可以去。

　　再次感谢你的邀请，希望你度过一个愉快的周末。

贝蒂谨上

Dear Betty,

　　Although I am sorry to hear that you can't come, I think it is right to keep the promise with your grandmother. I think you are a good girl. And it is convenient for me to arrange another plan to have dinner with my family. So enjoy the time with your grandmother.

　　Best wishes!

Yours sincerely,

Henry

亲爱的贝蒂：

　　虽然知道你不能来很遗憾，但是我认为你遵守和你外婆的约定帮她做家务是对的，你是个好女孩。再安排一次晚宴对我来说还是很方便的，希望你和你外婆过得开心。

　　祝好！

亨利谨上

Dear Betty,

I can understand that. And don't worry. We can have dinner next time. And if it is convenient for you, please call me. So we can make a proper time.

Best wishes!

Yours sincerely,

Henry

亲爱的贝蒂：

我能理解这个情况。不用担心，我们可以下次再一起吃晚饭。如果你方便的话，请打电话给我，这样我们就可以定个合适的时间。

祝好！

亨利谨上

读书笔记

Lesson 15 致歉信

如何写致歉信

a 直截了当地开始道歉，说明道歉的原因。

b 如果由于不得已而犯的错，要适当加以解释，但不要开脱自己的责任；如果确实是自己的疏忽，就应该诚恳地进行道歉，表明自己一定会改过。

c 说明自己打算如何补救自己的过错，提出补救措施和建议。

d 真心道歉，希望得到对方的谅解。

实用例句

1. I am writing to apologize that I can not participate in your birthday party tonight.

   我写这封信是为了向你道歉，我不能参加你今晚的生日派对了。

2. Please accept my apology for breaking your bike this afternoon.

   今天中午我弄坏了你的自行车，请接受我的道歉。

3. I deeply regret that I dirtied your clothes this morning.

   我很后悔今天早上弄脏了你的衣服。

4. I know my behavior is not inexcusable, and I am so sorry for...

   我知道我的行为是不容辩解的，我很抱歉……

5. This is my fault to...I will do everything I can to make some compensation.

   ……这是我的错，我将会做一切事情进行补偿。

6. I was so concentrated on my book and couldn't see you in front of me. I am sorry to knock over your coffee and dirty your clothes. I am so sorry to embarrass you.

   我看书太专注了，没有看见你站在我前面，于是打翻了你的咖啡，弄脏了你的衣服，我很抱歉让你尴尬。

7. You can call someone to fix that bike. And I will pay for the bill. Please call me at ×××. My name is ×××. I feel so sorry to do that. But I was not on purpose.

   你可以叫人来修理，我会付账单。请打电话给我，我的电话是×××，名字是×××。我感到很抱歉，但是我不是故意的。

8. If it is convenient for you, please give me your clothes and I will wash it and then give it back to you. Please give me your number.

如果方便的话，请把你的衣服给我，我会洗干净送还给你，请告诉我你的号码。

9. Please accept my sincere apology for doing that.

请接受我真挚的歉意。

10. I know it bothered you a lot and I will not do this anymore.

我知道这样做打扰到你，我保证不会再发生这样的事情了。

范本一 | 回信延迟的致歉

Dear Antony,

I'm sorry I am late to answer your letter. I'm so sorry to let you wait for such a long time.

Recently I was busy with my homework which the teacher asked me to finish as soon as possible. So I had a lot of things to do everyday. I was busy searching the information and writing the article. And then I forgot to reply your letter. I know you must be very worried about this.

I hope my reply can finally help you somehow. Please accept my sincere apology for doing that. I promise it will never happen again.

Yours sincerely,

Adam

亲爱的安东尼：

我很抱歉这么晚给你回信。让你久等了，我非常抱歉。

这几天我忙着写老师交给我的作业，因此我每天都有许多事情要做。我忙着查资料、写文章，所以忘记回复你的信件。我知道你一定等得很焦急。

希望我的回信没有耽误到你的事情。请接受我的道歉，下次绝对不会发生这样的情况了。

亚当谨上

Dear Adam,

I am so happy to receive your letter. You don't need to apologize. I know you must have your reason. I should call you at first. Actually your letter gives me a big help. Thank you very much.

Best wishes!

Yours sincerely,

Antony

亲爱的亚当：

收到你的来信我很高兴。你不用道歉，我知道你不回复我的信件一定是有原因的，我也应该事先打电话跟你确定一下，但是你的回信还是给了我很大的帮助。谢谢！

祝好！

安东尼谨上

Dear Adam,

I'm sorry to bother you. In fact my letter is not so important, but you still take time to respond to me. I am very happy. Thank you very much for your letter.

I wish you all the best.

Yours sincerely,

Antony

亲爱的亚当：

我很抱歉打扰到你了。其实我的信件并不是很重要，但是你还是抽空给我回复，我很高兴。非常感谢你的回信。

祝你一切顺利

安东尼谨上

范本二 | 不能赴约的致歉

Dear Antony,

I am writing this letter to apologize for missing the appointment that we should have a dinner on Sunday night.

I accepted your invitation, but on that day, came a notice from my boss to ask me to go on a business trip. There was no time for me to explain to you face to face. So I just made a phone call to cancel the appointment. I'm sorry about that. It is my fault to let you down. I hope we can make another appointment for dinner. It's my treat.

Here sending you my sincere apology.

Yours sincerely,

Adam

亲爱的安东尼：

我写这封信是为了向你道歉，我没有按照约定在星期天的晚上和你一起吃饭。

我接受了你的邀请，却在那天接到老板的通知要去出差。由于时间紧迫，我没有当面跟你解释，只是匆匆地打了个电话跟你取消了这次约会。很抱歉因为我的原因让你失望，我希望我们可以再约个时间吃顿饭，这顿我请客。

在这里送上我真挚的歉意。

亚当谨上

Dear Adam,

You don't have to feel sorry. You've told me on the phone why you can't come and I can understand that.

I know you are very busy, and always need to travel around on business. We have a lot of opportunities to have dinner together. We can make another appointment at the same time next week. If it's convenient, give me a call.

Wish you all the best!

Yours sincerely,

Antony

亲爱的亚当：

你不必觉得抱歉，你已经在电话里告诉我你失约的原因，我很理解。

我知道你的工作非常繁忙，需要经常出差。我们一起吃饭的机会还很多，我们可以把吃饭的时间定在下周同一时间。如果方便的话，打电话给我。

祝你一切顺利！

安东尼谨上

Dear Adam,

I am very happy to receive your letter. I hope you won't take it to your heart. It's no big deal. Sometimes I will also have this situation. I believe you can understand me too. Thank you very much for your letter to explain this thing.

Wish you all the best!

Yours sincerely,

Antony

亲爱的亚当：

收到你的来信我很高兴。希望你不要把这件事放在心上，没什么大不了的。我有时候也会有这样的情况，我相信你也是可以理解的。很感谢你来信说明这件事情。

祝你一切顺利！

安东尼谨上

范本三 | 未能完成任务的致歉

Dear teacher,

I'm sorry I didn't finish the article about the design of hotels in time. Because recently I was busy applying for an innovation fund project. And I should hand in the project plan before the deadline. I also participated in the chorus to represent our school to have a competition. And I needed to practice every day. So I had little time to write the article.

After the competition, I immediately began to write this article. But it's still a little bit late. Hope you can forgive me.

I'm very sorry. I promise I will finish the task next time.

Yours sincerely,

Adam

敬爱的老师：

我很抱歉我没有及时完成关于宾馆设计的文章。因为最近正在参加一个创业基金项目，需要在截止时间前上交项目计划书。我还要代表学校参加市里的合唱比赛，每天都要进行练习。所以写文章的时间很少。

比赛完了以后，我马上开始写这篇文章，但是还是有点迟。希望您原谅。

非常抱歉，下次我一定会按时完成您交代的任务。

亚当谨上

Dear Adam,

　　I know that you always have a lot of things to do. But remember that you should tell me in advance next assame, or I will assume you haven't finished your work and give you an "F" of this subject. You should pay attention next time.

Yours sincerely,
Antony

亲爱的亚当：

　　我知道你平时有很多事情要做，但是记得下次一定要先跟我说明，要不然我会以为你没有完成而给你低分的。下次注意。

安东尼谨上

Dear Adam,

　　Although I already knew the reason why you didn't finish your work, I still gave you a low score of this subject. Everyone needs to do so many things, so there is no reason you can hand in this work so late. It is not fair to other classmates who have handed it on time. I hope you can understand. Remember to tell me in advance next time.

Yours sincerely,
Antony

亲爱的亚当：

　　尽管我已经知道你没有完成作业的原因，但是我还是要给你一个比较低的分数。大家都有很多事情要做，不能你有事情要做就不扣你分，这对其他按时交作业的同学不公平，希望你理解。记得下次要提前告知我。

安东尼谨上

范本四 | 打扰某人的致歉

Dear Antony,

　　I am writing this letter to apologize to you. I feel really sorry to call you so late last night to ask you about the contract. Because yesterday I found that there was something wrong in contract needed to be modified as soon as possible. You are the person in charge, so I have to call you so late.

　　I'm very sorry to bother you. I hope you can forgive me.

Yours sincerely,
Adam

亲爱的安东尼：

我写这封信是为了向你道歉。昨天晚上那么晚打电话给你询问有关合约的事情，实在很抱歉。由于昨天才发现合约里的那个部分有些问题，需要马上修改，而你是主要负责人，我只能在那么晚打电话给你。

非常抱歉打扰你的正常休息，希望你见谅。

亚当谨上

Dear Adam,

Don't mind about this. I think I should say thank you for your timely warning that there was something wrong in the contract, to helped me avoid causing loss.

Best wishes!

Yours sincerely,
Antony

亲爱的亚当：

不要把这件事情放在心上。这件事还要多谢你及时发现了合约里存在的问题，避免发生损失。

祝好！

安东尼谨上

Dear Adam,

I can understand why you call me. I'm glad you can find the problem and put forward it. But I think, as one of the members of the project team, you should know how to modify. I believe you can handle it. What you need is more confidence. Hope you keep trying.

Best wishes!

Yours sincerely,
Antony

亲爱的亚当：

我能理解你这么做。我很高兴你能够发现这个问题并提出，但是我想，作为项目小组的成员之一，你应该知道怎么修改。我相信你自己能搞定的，你需要的是更多的信心。希望你继续加油。

祝好！

安东尼谨上

范本五 | 错怪某人的致歉

Dear Antony,

　　I'm sorry I blamed you on broking my bike. Because I saw my bike already broken when you pushed it yesterday, I thought you were the person who should be in charge of this. And I am sorry that also called you names very loudly. But then I knew that was not your fault, and in fact you were the person who wanted to help to repair the broken bike. I think I should apologize for my bad temper.

　　Please accept my sincere apology for doing that.

Yours sincerely,

Adam

亲爱的安东尼：

　　我很抱歉错怪你弄坏了我的自行车。因为昨天我看见你推着我的车的时候它已经坏了，所以我就认为是你把它弄坏的，还很大声地骂你。但是后来我才知道，原来你是要帮我修理已经坏掉的自行车。我为我的坏脾气道歉。

　　请你接受我真挚的歉意。

亚当谨上

Dear Adam,

　　I am not angry with you. I know you very well. This bike is your treasure. So I know why you were so angry with me. Never mind. I will forget what you said yesterday.

　　Best wishes!

Yours sincerely,

Antony

亲爱的亚当：

　　我没有生气。我了解你，这辆自行车是你的宝贝，也难怪你会这么生气。你不用介意，我没有把你昨天的话放在心上。

　　祝好！

安东尼谨上

Dear Adam,

Actually I was so sad about this. You called me names because of a bike. But I accept your apology. I think you should pay attention to your bad temper. So you can get well along with people around.

Yours sincerely,

Antony

亲爱的亚当：

说实话我很伤心，你竟然会为了一辆自行车和我吵架。我接受你的道歉，但是我希望你改改你的坏脾气，这样才能跟周围的人更好地相处。

祝好！

安东尼谨上

读书笔记

Lesson 16　节日祝福信

如何写节日祝福信

ⓐ直接表达对对方节日的问候和祝福。

ⓑ说明这个节日的特殊含义，表达自己的感情和感想。

ⓒ再次送上自己最真挚的祝福。

实用例句

1. Happy new year! Please accept my best wishes for a very enjoyable holiday.

   新年快乐！请接受我对这个愉快节日的祝福。

2. Merry Christmas! It is a big festival for people celebrating the reunion.

   圣诞快乐！这真是个庆祝团圆的好日子。

3. I wish you can have a enjoyable holiday and have a good fortune in the following days.

   我祝你有个愉快的假期，接下来的日子都有好运相伴。

4. Let's celebrate the big holiday and wish you all the dreams come true.

   让我们一起庆祝这个节日，祝愿你美梦成真。

5. I hope this New Year can bring you happiness and good luck.

   我希望你在新年里可以幸福快乐好运。

6. Happy Mother's Day! Wish you always be happy, young and beautiful. You are the most beautiful woman in my eyes.

   母亲节快乐！希望妈妈永远快乐、年轻、美丽，你永远都是我眼中最美的女人。

7. Happy Teachers' Day! May you be happy and healthy forever!

   教师节快乐！祝愿老师永远快乐健康。

8. I am so happy to send you the best wishes for health and happiness.

   我很高兴能够送上我最美好的祝福，祝愿你健康快乐。

9. I hope we can have the big holiday together next year.

   我希望我们可以来年再一起共度佳节。

10. Thank you for your concern and caring. Wish you all the best and have a good life.

    谢谢你的关心和照顾。愿你一切都好，有个美好的生活。

范本一 | 新年祝福

Dear Catherine,

New Year is coming soon. I am so happy to celebrate the holiday with you. Thank you for always helping me. Wish the New Year will bring you health and happiness. And wish you all dreams come true.

Happy New Year!

Yours sincerely,

Denise

亲爱的凯瑟琳：

转眼新的一年到了。能与你一起欢庆，我很高兴，谢谢你一直以来对我的帮助。祝你新的一年，梦想成真，身体健康，生活愉快！

新年快乐！

丹尼斯谨上

Dear Denise,

Happy New Year to you too! I am happy to receive your letter. And I also wish you happy all the time.

Yours sincerely,

Catherine

亲爱的丹尼斯：

也祝你新年快乐！我很高兴收到你的来信，也希望你能永远开心。

凯瑟琳谨上

Dear Denise,

It is a big holiday for all of us. Happy New Year! May you have a joyous holiday with your family and the New Year will bring you happiness and success.

Yours sincerely,

Catherine

亲爱的丹尼斯：

　　这对于我们来说是个盛大的节日。新年快乐！希望你和你的家人能度过愉快的节日，也希望新的一年会给你带来幸福和成功。

凯瑟琳谨上

范本二｜圣诞祝福

Dear Catherine,

　　Here comes the Christmas Day. And Merry Christmas! Every year we will go back to our hometown and celebrate the holiday with friends, families and you! It is a wonderful thing to have a good time with all of you. I wish you can all have a good life and healthy body.

Yours sincerely,
Denise

亲爱的凯瑟琳：

　　圣诞节就要来了，圣诞快乐！每年我们都回到我们的家乡与我们的朋友，亲人，还有你一起庆祝这个美好的节日，能够和你们一起度过这个节日真的很棒。希望你们都有美好的生活，健康的身体。

丹尼斯谨上

Dear Denise,

　　Merry Christmas, my friend! I am glad to hear from you. I am also very happy to have the good time with you. And I also hope you can have a better life too.

Yours sincerely,
Catherine

亲爱的丹尼斯：

　　亲爱的朋友，圣诞快乐！我很高兴收到你的来信，我也很高兴能和你一起度过这个美好的时刻。我也祝你有更好的生活。

凯瑟琳谨上

Dear Denise,

　　Merry Christmas! Let's make an appointment to drink a toast on Christmas Day to wish we can be both healthy and happy!

Yours sincerely,
Catherine

亲爱的丹尼斯:

圣诞快乐！让我们约定在圣诞节那天一起举杯庆祝，祝我们身体健康，生活愉快！

凯瑟琳谨上

范本三 | 母亲节祝福

Dear Mom,

Tomorrow is Mother's Day. Happy Mother's Day! Please accept my sincere wishes for you. Thank you for raising me up and giving me so much love and caring. I love you forever. You are the most beautiful woman in my eyes. I hope you can be young and beautiful forever.

I love you!

Yours sincerely,
Catherine

亲爱的妈妈:

明天就是母亲节了，祝您母亲节快乐，请收下我最真挚的祝福。谢谢您养育了我，给了我如此多的爱和关怀，我永远爱您。您永远是我眼中最美的女人，我祝您永远年轻，美丽。

我爱您！

凯瑟琳谨上

Dear Catherine,

Thank you for your letter. I am happy to hear that. This is the most wonderful thing in my life to receive the letter from my daughter and to know how much she loves me. Thank you, my sweet heart.

Yours sincerely,
Mom

亲爱的凯瑟琳:

谢谢你的来信，我很高兴收到这封信。我这一生中最棒的事就是收到我女儿的节日祝福信，告诉我她有多爱我。谢谢你，我的宝贝！

妈妈

Dear Catherine,

I am so excited to hear from you. I think my daughter has grown up. I am so proud of you and I am happy to be your mom. Thank you for your letter. This is the best gift for Mother's Day.

Yours sincerely,
Mom

亲爱的凯瑟琳：

收到你的来信我很激动。我想我的女儿已经长大了，我很为你自豪，作为你的母亲我很高兴。谢谢你的这封信，这是我母亲节收到最好的礼物。

妈妈

范本四｜教师节祝福

Dear Miss Li,

Teachers' Day is coming soon. And I should say Happy Teachers' Day to you.

You are a very good teacher. You always give me so much concern and teach me so many things. And you also tell us what is right and what is wrong. And ask us to do the right thing. I don't know how to express my gratitude.

So please accept my sincere wishes. I hope you can be in good health and have a happy life.

Yours sincerely,
Catherine

亲爱的李老师：

教师节即将来临，我想说：祝您教师节快乐。

您是一位好老师。您经常给予我关心和爱护，教会了我很多东西，告诉我们什么是对的，什么是错的，教我们正确的人生观和价值观，我不知道该怎么表达我的谢意。

所以请接受我最真挚的祝福，祝老师身体健康，生活幸福。

凯瑟琳谨上

Dear Catherine,

Thank you for your letter to send your best wishes to me. I am so happy to receive this letter. I think being a teacher is a wonderful thing because I can get reward from you. Not expecting for something, I just want to be remembered. To see this letter is a good reward for me.

Yours sincerely,
Miss Li

亲爱的凯瑟琳：

　　谢谢你的来信祝福。我很高兴能够收到你的来信，我认为作为一个老师是一件很棒的事情，因为常常会有回报，并不是说收到什么东西，而是想要被记得。你的这封信让我觉得有了很好的回报。

李老师

Dear Catherine,

　　Thank you for your letter. This letter makes me so happy that I am sure being a teacher is a good choice for me. I will keep doing what I am doing, and teach what I have learnt to my students. Thank you very much to give me the wishes.

　　And wish you all the best too.

Yours sincerely,
Miss Li

亲爱的凯瑟琳：

　　谢谢你的来信。这封信让我很高兴，也让我相信选择作为一名老师是正确的选择。我将会继续我正在做的事情，把我所学教给我的学生。非常感谢你给我的祝福。

　　也祝你一切顺利！

李老师

主要节日词汇一览表

- ◆ 1月1日元旦(New Year's Day)
- ◆ 2月14日情人节(Valentine's Day)
- ◆ 3月8日国际妇女节(International Women' Day)
- ◆ 3月12日中国植树节(China Arbor Day)
- ◆ 3月14日白色情人节(White Day)
- ◆ 4月1日愚人节(April Fools' Day)
- ◆ 4月5日清明节(Tomb-sweeping Day)
- ◆ 5月1日国际劳动节(International Labour Day)
- ◆ 5月4日中国青年节(Chinese Youth Day)
- ◆ 5月8日世界红十字日(World Red-Cross Day)
- ◆ 5月12日国际护士节(International Nurse Day)
- ◆ 5月15日国际家庭日(International Family Day)

- 5月17日世界电信日(World Telecommunications Day)

- 5月20日全国学生营养日(National Students' Nutrition Day)

- 5月23日国际牛奶日(International Milk Day)

- 5月31日世界无烟日(World No-Smoking Day)

- 6月1日国际儿童节(International Children's Day)

- 6月5日世界环境日(International Environment Day)

- 6月6日全国爱眼日(National Eye-Care Day)

- 6月17日世界防治荒漠化和干旱日(World Day to Combat Desertification)

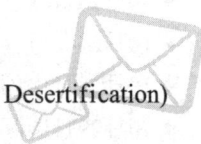

- 6月23日国际奥林匹克日(International Olympic Day)

- 6月25日全国土地日(National Land Day)

- 6月26日国际禁毒日(International Day Against Drug Abuse and Illicit Trafficking)

- 7月1日中国共产党诞生日(Anniversary of the Founding of the Chinese Communist Party)

- 7月1日国际建筑日(International Architecture Day)

- 7月7日中国人民抗日战争纪念日(Chinese People's Anti-Japanese War Anniversary)

- 7月11日世界人口日(World Population Day)

- 8月1日中国人民解放军建军节(Army Day)

- 8月12日国际青年节(International Youth Day)

- 9月8日国际扫盲日(International Anti-Illiteracy Day)

- 9月10日中国教师节(Teacher's Day)

- 9月16日中国脑健康日(Chinese Brain Health Day)

- 9月20日全国爱牙日(National Love Teeth Day)

- 9月21日世界停火日(World Cease-fire Day)

- 9月27日世界旅游日(World Tourism Day)

- 10月1日中华人民共和国国庆节(National Day)

- 10月1日国际音乐日(International Music Day)

- 10月1日国际老年人日(International Day of Older Persons)

- 10月4日世界动物日(World Animal Day)

- 10月5日世界教师日(World Teachers' Day)(联合国教科文组织确立)

- 10月8日全国高血压日(National High Blood Pressure)

- 10月9日世界邮政日(World Post Day)

- 10月10日世界精神卫生日(World Mental Health Day)

- 10月14日世界标准日(World Standards Day)
- 10月15日国际盲人节(International Day of the Blind)
- 10月15日世界农村妇女日(World Rural Women's Day)
- 10月16日世界粮食日(World Food Day)
- 10月17日国际消除贫困日(International Day for the Eradication of Poverty)
- 10月24日联合国日(United Nations Day)
- 10月24日世界发展新闻日(World Development Information Day)
- 10月28日中国男性健康日(Chinese Men's Health Day)
- 10月29日国际生物多样性日(International Biodiversity Day)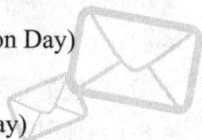
- 10月31日万圣节(Halloween)
- 11月8日中国记者节(Journalists' Day)
- 11月9日消防宣传日(Fire Awareness Day)
- 11月14日世界糖尿病日(World Diabetes Day)
- 11月17日国际大学生节(International Students' Day)
- 11月25日国际消除对妇女的暴力日(International Day For the Elimination of Violence against Women)
- 12月1日世界艾滋病日(World AIDS Day)
- 12月3日世界残疾人日(World Disabled Day)
- 12月4日全国法制宣传日(National Legal Publicity Day)
- 12月9日世界足球日(World Football Day)
- 12月25日圣诞节(Christmas Day)
- 12月29日国际生物多样性日(International Biological Diversity Day)
- 1月最后一个星期日国际麻风节(International Leprosy Day)
- 春分月圆后的第一个星期日复活节(Easter)(有可能是3月22~4月25日间的任一天)
- 5月第二个星期日母亲节(Mother's Day)
- 6月第三个星期日父亲节(Father's Day)
- 9月第三个星期二国际和平日(International Peace Day)
- 9月第三个星期六全国国防教育日(National Defense Education Day)
- 9月第四个星期日国际聋人节(International Day of the Deaf)
- 10月的第一个星期一世界住房日(World Habitat Day)
- 10月的第二个星期一加拿大感恩节(Thanksgiving Day)
- 10月第二个星期三国际减轻自然灾害日(International Day for Natural Disaster Reduction)
- 10月第二个星期四世界爱眼日(World Sight Day)

- ◆ 11月最后一个星期四美国感恩节(Thanksgiving Day)
- ◆ 农历节日
- ◆ 农历正月初一春节(The Spring Festival)
- ◆ 农历正月十五元宵节(The Lantern Festival)
- ◆ 农历五月初五端午节(The Dragon-Boat Festival)
- ◆ 农历七月初七乞巧节（中国情人节）(Double-Seventh Day)
- ◆ 农历八月十五中秋节(The Mid-Autumn Festival)
- ◆ 农历九月初九重阳节(The Double Ninth Festival)
- ◆ 农历腊月初八腊八节(The Laba Rice Porridge Festival)

读书笔记

Lesson 17 求助信

如何写求助信

ⓐ 首先问候对方，简要说明自己的要求，让对方能够很快知道你的写信目的。

ⓑ 清楚地告诉对方需要对方做的事，并恳请对方能够给予帮助。

ⓒ 表示感谢，并祝福对方。

实用例句

1. Thank you for your attention. I am writing to ask you to help me write a recommendation.

   谢谢您的关注。我写这封信的目的是想请你帮我写一封推荐信。

2. I appreciate your time and your effort. Thank you very much.

   这一定会花费你不少时间和精力，我非常感激。

3. If you need more information, please call me at 223-321-3456

   如果你需要更多信息，请联系我，我的电话是223-321-3456

4. Recently I have been writing a paper about tourism management of the hotels. So I need some information about the hotel. I wonder whether you can give me a help.

   最近我在写一篇关于饭店旅游管理的文章，所以需要一些关于饭店的信息，不知道你是否能帮我个忙。

5. I have worked for the company for about five years and I appreciate your concern and care. And recently I have been promoted to be the manager of the department, so I want to discuss the possibility of a pay raise.

   我在这个公司已经工作五年了，我很感激公司对我的关心和帮助。最近我刚升职为部门主管，我想和您讨论一下我的加薪问题。

6. I want to ask you to lend some money to me, because I don't have enough money to go on my business.

   我想问你借点钱，因为我的钱不够做生意。

7. Can you tell me who I should write to in your company? And if it is convenient for you, can you give me more detailed information about your

company, so I can well prepare the interview.

你能告诉我信写给你们公司谁吗？如果方便的话，请多告诉我一点你们公司的信息，这样我就能更好地准备我的面试。

8. A few days ago, I have read a book which mentions a book named *The Seven Habits of the Highly Effective People.* So I want to ask you if you can borrow the book from your library for me.

几天前，我在一本书上看到了一本叫《高效能人士的七个习惯》，所以我想问你是否可以帮我向你们图书馆借一下这本书。

9. You are the master of this field, so I need some advices from you. Would you please give me some materials about management?

你是这方面的专家，我需要你的建议。你能给我一些有关管理的材料吗？

10. Thank you very much for your attention. Wish you all the best!

非常感谢。希望你一切都好！

范本一 | 请求借钱

Dear Annie,

I am writing to you to ask if you can lend me some money.

I have also already spent a lot of money on my business. Recently my child has been badly ill, and I have spent all the money we have to pay for the medicine. And so I don't have enough money to pay for the medicine for my baby. I need to ask you to do me a favor. I will appreciate that.

Wish you all the best!

Yours sincerely,

Mary

亲爱的安妮：

我写信的目的是想向你借点钱。

我已经将很多钱投资到了我的生意中去了，最近，我的孩子病得很厉害，我已经花了我所有的钱来支付医药费，我已经没有足够的钱来支付医药费。我想请你帮忙，我会感激你的。

祝你一切顺利！

玛丽谨上

Dear Mary,

I am so sorry to hear that. I would like to lend you some money. And please tell me how much you need. I think nothing is important than baby. I hope you can get through this. Wish your baby will get better.

Best wishes!

Yours sincerely,

Annie

亲爱的玛丽：

听到这个消息，我很遗憾。我愿意借你钱，请告诉我你需要多少，我想没有什么事情比孩子更重要了。希望你们能渡过这个难关，也希望你们的孩子早日健康。

祝好！

安妮谨上

Dear Mary,

I am so sorry to tell you that I have no money to lend you, because I have spent all my money to do the investment. Now I have no extra money to lend you. But I will try to ask someone else. Maybe they can lend you the money. Don't worry! You can get through this. If there is something else I can do, please let me know.

Wish you all the best!

Yours sincerely,

Annie

亲爱的玛丽：

我非常抱歉，我没有钱可以借给你，因为我把我的钱都拿去做投资了，没有多余的钱，但是我会帮你问问别人，也许他们可以把钱借给你。你不要担心，你能渡过这个难关的。如果有什么其他事情我能帮忙的，请告诉我。

祝你一切顺利！

安妮谨上

范本二 | 请求写介绍信

Dear Annie,

I am writing this letter to ask you to help me write a letter of recommendation. I hope you can introduce me to apply for the position of assistant of the general manager.

I've been working for this company for two years as a secretary of the manager of the department. I have rich working experience. And my major is administrative management. I have good knowledge of this major, and I also have a good ability of writing and expression. I hope you can write a recommendation for me. I appreciate your time and your effort. Thank you very much.

Best wishes!

Yours sincerely,
Mary

亲爱的安妮：

我写这封信是想请你帮我写一封介绍信，希望可以介绍我去应聘总经理助理这个工作。

我已经做了两年的部门经理秘书工作，我有很丰富的工作经验。而且我的专业是行政管理，我具有很强的专业知识，有很好的写作能力和表达能力，希望能够得到你的推荐。这一定需要花费很多时间和精力，我非常感激。

祝好！

玛丽谨上

Dear Mary,

I am happy to receive your letter. It is my pleasure to write this letter for you. You are a good staff. And I hope you can get the position, and do the work better. I believe you can do this job well.

Best wishes!

Yours sincerely,
Annie

亲爱的玛丽：

我很高兴收到你的来信，我也很乐意帮你写这封推荐信。你是一名非常优秀的员工，希望你可以得到这个工作，把工作做得更好。我相信你能做好的。

祝好！

安妮谨上

Dear Mary,

I am so sorry to tell you that the position you want to apply has been filled. And I think there is no need to write this recommendation. But I think you are an excellent employee in our company. I believe you can have another chance. At I will write this letter for you!

Best wishes!

Yours sincerely,

Annie

亲爱的玛丽：

我很遗憾地告诉你，你申请的这个职位已经有合适的人选了，所以我觉得已经没有必要写推荐信了。但是我认为你是一名非常优秀的员工，你会有下次机会，那时我会再为你写推荐信。

祝好！

安妮谨上

范本三 | 请求寄书

Dear Annie,

I need your help to send me a book named *The Seven Habits of the Highly Effective People*. Recently I have seen some information on the internet about the book, and I like it very much. And I heard that you had finished the book. So would you please send it to me? Then I don't need to buy it.

Thank you very much. And I will pay the fee of the delivery.

Yours sincerely,

Mary

亲爱的安妮：

我需要你帮我寄那本《高效能人士的七个习惯》。最近我在网上看到一些关于这本书的信息，我很喜欢。听说你有这本书，并且已经看完了，所以你可不可以把它寄给我看看？那样我就不用再买一本。

非常感谢，我会付邮资的。

玛丽谨上

Dear Mary,

I would like to send you this book. I think it is wonderful and tell us a lot of good advice. And I think it can also give you some feelings and opinions about life and how to be effective people. Hope you like it.

Best wishes!

Yours sincerely,

Annie

亲爱的玛丽：

我可以把这本书寄给你看看。我觉得这本书非常棒，告诉了我们很多很好的建议。我想它也能给你一些关于生活以及关于如何能成为高效人士的感受和想法。希望你喜欢。

祝好！

安妮谨上

Dear Mary,

I am sorry to tell you that I have donated this book to the poor. I think it is a good book and we should share it with others. So when the volunteers asked me if I could donate some books, I gave them all the books I had read. I am sorry.

Best wishes!

Yours sincerely,

Annie

亲爱的玛丽：

我很抱歉告诉你，我已经把书捐给了贫困区的人们。我认为这是一本很好的书，值得与他人一起分享，所以当志愿者们问我是否有书愿意捐出时，我就把我读过的所有书都捐出去了。我很抱歉。

祝好！

安妮谨上

范本四 | 请求买书

Dear Annie,

Thank you for your attention. I want to ask you to help me buy a book in the book store near your home. It names *The Seven Habits of the Highly Effective People*.

I heard you said that the book in the store near your home was much cheaper than other stores. So I wonder if you can buy me one. I will appreciate that.

Best wishes!

Yours sincerely,

Mary

亲爱的安妮：

你好！我想让你帮我在你家附近的书店买一本叫《高效能人士的七个习惯》的书。

我听到你说这本书在你家附近的书店卖得比其他店里的要便宜，所以想问你是否可以帮我买一本。非常感谢。

祝好！

玛丽谨上

Dear Mary,

I am happy to hear from you. It's my pleasure to buy you the book. As I told you that this book is much cheaper in that store, and the quality of the book is also very good. And I think you will love it.

Best wishes!

Yours sincerely,

Annie

亲爱的玛丽：

我很高兴收到你的来信，我很乐意帮你买这本书。正如我告诉你的，这家店里的这本书很便宜，而且质量也很好。我想你会喜欢的。

祝好！

安妮谨上

Dear Mary,

I am so sorry to tell you that I am on a vacation in Thailand. And I will stay here for about two weeks. So if you are eager to buy the book, you should ask someone else. Or you could wait for me about two weeks. I am so sorry to tell you that.

Best wishes!

Yours sincerely,

Annie

亲爱的玛丽：

　　我很抱歉告诉你，我现在在泰国度假，大概要待半个月左右。如果你很急着买这本书的话，你就要问问其他人是否方便帮你买，如果不急的话，就等两个星期后我回去再给你买。我很抱歉。

　　祝好！

安妮谨上

读书笔记

Lesson 18　表扬信

如何写表扬信

表扬信是因为某件事对某个机构或人提出表扬的一种信函，写表扬信一般遵循下列步骤：

ⓐ 开头顶格称呼，写上个人姓名，如果表扬对象为一个部门或群体，可以用"Dear All"来称呼。

ⓑ 主题部分条理清晰，写明事情发生的时间、地点、所发生的具体事情、事情的结果以及影响、表现出怎样的好品德、并且值得我们学习。表扬信的主题部分应该遵循先叙述事实再进行表扬的基本结构，使人一目了然。

ⓒ 结尾署名。

实用例句

1. I am writing to express my thanks for...

我写这封信是为了表达对……的感谢之情。

2. I am writing to express my sincere praise for...

我写这封信是表达我对……诚挚的赞扬。

3. Thank you so much for the help you gave me.

非常感谢您给予我的帮助。

4. On behalf of my whole family, I would like to praise John for...

我谨代表我全家表扬约翰……

5. Your behavior is very much appreciated by each one of us.

我们每个人都非常欣赏你这样的行为。

6. Please accept my praise, now and always.

请接受我的赞扬，直到永远。

7. Such behavior should be glorified and learned by the public.

这种行为应该得到赞美并值得大众学习。

8. I appreciate your selfless donation.

我欣赏你无私奉献的精神。

9. I really admire your generous dedication.

我敬佩你慷慨奉献的品质。

10. I feel most obliged to thank you again.

我对你感激不尽。

📧 范本一 | 表扬信（1）

Dear Joy,

    I am writing to thank you for taking care of me when I was in hospital. The day before yesterday, I had an unfortunate accident on my way home. I was hit by a car and my knees were hurt, then I was sent to the nearest hospital to be given treatment. You helped me taking rehabilitation every day and looked after me carefully. The intimate service helped me recover more quickly. I would like to convey in this letter my heartfelt thanks to you for your enthusiasm.

    Please accept my praise, now and always.

Best regards,

Stella

亲爱的乔依：

    我写这封信给你是想谢谢你在我住院期间给予我的照顾。前天我在回家的路上遭遇了一起不幸的车祸，我被车撞了，膝盖受伤，然后被送去了最近的医院接受治疗。这几天你每天帮助我做恢复训练并细心照顾我，这样贴心的照顾帮助我更快恢复了。我想用这封信来表达我对你热心帮助的衷心感谢。

    请接受我对你的表扬，直到永远。

致敬

斯蒂拉谨上

Dear Stella,

    I am very happy to receive your letter. You are so nice to remember such small things. It is my responsibility as a patient care to look after you well. Your letter would encourage me to do my work better and better in the future.

    If you need my help one day, please don't hesitate to contact me.

Yours sincerely,

Joy

亲爱的斯蒂拉:

　　收到你的来信我非常高兴。你真的很细心，还记得这种小事。作为护工，我的责任就是照顾好你。你的来信将会鼓励我在将来越来越好地完成工作。

　　如果你哪天需要我的帮助，不要犹豫，请直接联系我。

乔依谨上

Dear Stella,

　　I greatly appreciate your letter for praising my performance. I just did what I should do. It is my duty to help patients in the hospital. I feel positive pleasure to see the patients recover and have a new life after leaving hospital. All this reflects the value of my own life. I am really excited to receive your praise letter, because it is an affirmation to my work. I will pay all my enthusiasm into my job and help more people to have health!

Yours sincerely,
Joy

亲爱的斯蒂拉:

　　我非常高兴收到你表扬我工作表现的来信。我只是做了我应该做的事而已，帮助医院里的病患是我的职责。看到病人们康复，出院后拥有新生活，我感到由衷的高兴。这些都反映了我的人生价值。收到你的来信我真的非常激动，因为这是对我工作的肯定。我将会把我所有的热情灌注于我的工作中并帮助更多的人获得健康!

乔恩谨上

范本二 | 表扬信（2）

Dear John,

　　I am writing to thank you for returning my lost wallet. Last Friday when I was taking a walk along the river, I lost my wallet there. After I came back home, I found that I could not find my wallet. There was a large sum of money in it, because I had planned to buy a new computer. I felt worried and returned to look for it along the river again and again. Before you returned the wallet to me, I was really worried to death. It is so nice of you! It is great to your credit that you returned money back, and your honesty should be praised.

$100 is enclosed here. Please accept my thanks!

Best regards,

Kevin

亲爱的约翰:

我专程写信来感谢你将我丢失的钱包还给我。上周五当我在河边散步时，我丢失了钱包，回到家后才发现钱包不见了。钱包里有一大笔钱，因为我正准备买台新电脑。我非常着急并且返回沿着河边找了一遍又一遍。在你把钱包还来之前，我真是急死了！你人真是太好了！你拾金不昧是非常难能可贵的，值得表扬。

随信附赠100美元。请务必接受我的感谢之情！

致敬

凯文

Dear Kevin,

I am glad to receive your letter. Actually, it is just a piece of cake. I lift a finger to return the wallet to you because there was detailed address in your visiting card. I was brought up not pocketing the money I had picked up, because it belongs to other people, and I know the owner must be worried when losing such a huge amount of money.

I must return the $100 to you because I would not give the wallet back to you if I have mercenary motives. Please give it to someone who needs it worse than I do.

Yours sincerely,

John

亲爱的凯文:

我很高兴收到你的来信。实际上，这只是一件小事，因为你的名片上有详细地址，所以还钱包给你只是举手之劳。我从小就被教育要拾金不昧，因为是别人的东西，而且我知道当失主丢失这么大笔钱的时候一定非常着急。

我必须要将100块还给你，我如果是贪图钱财的话就不会把钱包还给你了，请将这笔钱赠予更需要的人吧！

谨启！

约翰

Dear Kevin,

I am so happy that such a little thing can win me praise! That's so nice of you to send me the letter. I just did what I should do and understood the owner's mood. It is a pity that if the wallet can not be found or taken away by someone.

In addition, you should learn to keep this kind of valuables in a safe place after this issue.

I feel so joyful to receive your praise! Thank you for your $100.

Yours sincerely,

John

亲爱的凯文：

我很高兴这样一件小事也会赢得表扬！你真是太客气了还写信给我，我只是做了我该做的事情，而且我理解失主的心情。如果钱包再也找不到或者被别人捡去了会非常遗憾的。

另外，经过这件事后你应该要将如此贵重的东西放置到安全的地方。

收到你的表扬我感到非常开心！谢谢你的100美元。

谨启！

约翰

范本三 | 表扬信（3）

Dear manager,

I am a newsman, so I often need to travel around. Every time I travel here I would choose your hotel without any hesitation because the service here is so careful and makes me comfortable. I am writing to praise your outstanding service and attitude for customers. The waiters and waitresses are so kind and warm-hearted that they always take everything into account for me. They remember my name and send me fresh fruits and food from restaurant. It is almost the same as at home when I live here.

Hope your hotel will be more prosperous in the future!

Sincerely yours,

Jim

经理你好：

我是一名新闻记者，所以需要经常四处出差。每一次出差到这里我都会毫不犹豫地选择你们的酒店，因为这里的服务实在是太细心了，令我感到非常舒适。我专程写信来表扬你们对顾客出色的服务和态度。服务员特别贴心和热心，总是替我考虑许多事情，他们记得我的名字而且会给我送来餐厅新鲜的水果和食物，住在这里就像在家一样。

希望你们酒店未来发展更加出色！

谨启！
杰姆

Dear Jim,

Thank you very much for your letter! We feel greatly honored to be praised by you. The service purpose of our hotel is to make customers feel at home, so we are trying best to consider your needs. We can only expand hugely by putting us in the position of customers. Your appreciation of our work will encourage us to make our service step further. We will provide the most comfortable and careful service as usual.

If you have any suggestion, please advise us.

Thank you!

Best regards,
Manager Tom

亲爱的杰姆：

非常感谢您的来信！收到您的表扬我们深感荣幸。我们酒店的服务宗旨就是令顾客像在家一样舒适，所以我们尽最大努力考虑客户的需求，只有站在客户的角度服务我们才能发展壮大。我们的工作受到您的肯定鼓励我们会将服务做到更上一层楼，我们将会一如既往提供最舒适和最细致的服务。

如果您对我们的工作有什么建议，请尽管提出来。

谢谢！

珍重
经理：汤姆

Dear Jim,

I am happy all the morning as I received the letter from you. You are so kind and attentive! Thank you very much for choosing our hotel as your residence. What we should do is creating an environment for you to live comfortable. You are an old customer of our hotel, so the waiters and waitresses know you prefer fresh fruits than juice. Considering customers' requirements and preference is our duty. We feel joy that you are satisfied with our service.

We will offer the first class of service.

Best regards,
Manager Tom

亲爱的杰姆：

收到您的来信我一早上都非常高兴。您人真是太好太细心了！特别感谢您选择我们酒店作为下榻之所。我们要做的就是为你们创造舒适的环境。您是我们酒店的老顾客，所以服务员知道您喜欢新鲜水果而不是果汁。考虑顾客的需求和喜好是我们的责任，您对我们的服务满意令我们感到非常开心。

我们将会为顾客提供一流的服务。

珍重

经理：汤姆

范本四 | 表扬信（4）

Dear Leaders,

I am writing to praise the student named Jay who is in 8th grade in your school. Yesterday I forgot to turn off the gas when I left home in a hurry to the supermarket to buy some vegetables. It was Joy who went past my home and found something was unusual in my house, then the student called policeman to come to put out the fire. Fortunately, fire crews extinguished the blaze before it could spread to more pumps. Only my kitchen was burned.

The guy is so kind and careful! I am so grateful for him to find the fire, avoiding losses. As a middle school student, he has courage and on outstanding judgment. I can hardly express how grateful I am for his help.

Thanks to Jay!

Best wishes,
Michelle

尊敬的校领导：

我写信给您专程表扬你们学校初二学生杰伊。昨天我匆忙离开家去超市买蔬菜的时候忘记关掉煤气，后来杰伊路过我家发现了异常，然后打电话叫来消防扑灭了火。幸运的是，火势并未蔓延，只有厨房被烧毁。

　　这个孩子真的热心又仔细！我非常感谢他发现了火情并且让我避免了损失。作为一个中学生，他有勇气和出色的判断力，对于他的帮助我简直无法用言语表达。

　　谢谢杰伊！

诚挚的问候
米歇尔

Dear Michelle,

　　We were so unexpected to receive your letter and then proved it to Jay. He didn't tell anything about the fire when he went to school. We are proud of this student who is outstanding but modest. He said that day when he went on the road, he suddenly smelt the burning air and found fire from the window of your kitchen. He made the prompt decision to call the police at that time.

　　We decide to praise him in the morning assembly. This kind of spirit is well worth being learned by other students too.

　　Thank you for your letter!

Best wishes!
Principle
Jack

亲爱的米歇尔：

　　我们收到你的来信很意外，然后向杰伊求证了。他来到学校后只字未提火灾的事情，我们很骄傲学校有这样出色而谦虚的学生。他说那天他走在路上，突然闻到了焦味并且透过你家厨房窗户发现里面有火苗，他当机立断报了警。

　　我们决定在校晨会上表扬他，这种精神也非常值得别的学生学习。

　　感谢您的来信！

诚挚的祝福您！
校长：杰克

Lesson 19 批评抱怨信

如何写批评抱怨信

ⓐ 批评抱怨信在格式上与别的信件没有什么大的差别，同样是开头问候，主题陈述再加结尾签字。

ⓑ 批评抱怨信的主题内容需要层次分明，因为表达的内容较多，所以基本框架为：提出抱怨的内容，陈述原因，客观评论后结尾加上建议意见。

实用例句

1. When we came to examine the goods which were dispatched by you, we found that...

   当我们检查你们发来的货物时，发现……

2. The quality of this goods is far from being satisfactory.

   这批货物的质量远不能令人满意。

3. We have received a lot of complaints from our customers who is concerning the quality.

   我们已经收到好多客户关于产品质量问题的抱怨。

4. The goods we ordered from you have not been delivered yet.

   我们所定的货物至今为止还未发货。

5. We would be glad if you deal with the matter at once and let us know the reason of delay.

   希望你们立刻着手处理这件事，并告诉我们货物延误的原因。

6. The goods you send to me is out of my expectation.

   你们寄来的货物令我大失所望。

7. In view of the inconvenience that this has caused, I feel you must...

   鉴于这给我们带来的不便，我认为你们必须……

8. Your prompt attention will be appreciated.

   如果你们能及时处理这件事的话，我们将不胜感激。

9. We trust you can understand that we expect the compensation for our damaged goods.

   相信你们能理解我方要求对损坏货物进行赔偿的要求。

10. I hope that the waiters would improve their attitude and quality of service in the future.

我希望这些服务员将来能提高自身服务态度和素质。

范本一｜学生食堂问题抱怨批评

Dear Jane,

I am writing to reflect some problems in the students' dining hall and hope you can find a way to solve them:

1. Waste is a serious problem in the dining room. Many students can not eat all their foods and pour away a large proportion of foods. I feel very worried, because food is very precious to us.

2. Many students speak very loudly during eating. This kind of behavior is impolite and unhealthy.

3. Most of the students are picky eaters. It has a harmful effect on body growth.

My suggestion is to make some rules to restrict students' food waste. The teachers should instruct good eating manners.

Best regards,

Blair

亲爱的简：

我想反映几个有关学生食堂的问题，并希望你能找到解决方案：

1.食堂浪费现象特别严重。许多学生吃不完饭，倒掉大部分食物，我感到非常痛心，因为粮食对我们来说非常珍贵。

2.许多学生在就餐期间大声讲话。这种习惯是不礼貌且有害健康的。

3.大部分学生非常挑食。这对身体发育是有害的。

我的建议是对于食物浪费现象制定一些针对性的规定，老师应该引导学生养成良好的就餐习惯。

诚挚的祝福

布莱尔

Dear Blair,

Thank you for reflecting such practical problems about the students' dining hall to me. After discussing with some leaders of school, we will issue some solutions:

1. We decide to issue the rules to restrain the students' behavior of waste. Besides, we will organize students to watch related films to remind them that the food is so value to us.

2. The teachers should play important roles to supervise and guide the students to develop good eating manners.

3. We will communicate with our cook who is in charge of the dishes to develop balanced diet to help students grow healthily.

We will pay close attention to the condition in the dining hall and develop the solutions according to the circumstance in the future.

Best wishes,

Jane

亲爱的布莱尔：

感谢你向我反映学生食堂中的实际问题。在与校领导商量了之后，我们决定出台以下措施：

1.我们决定列出一些具体规则限制学生的浪费现象。另外，我们将会组织学生观看相关电影，从而提醒他们食物对我们来说是如此珍贵。

2.老师应该在教导约束学生养成良好就餐方面发挥重要作用。

3.我们将会与负责食堂餐饮的厨师沟通，让他制定出营养均衡的配餐，帮助学生健康成长。

我们将会密切关注食堂环境并且及时根据情况制定相关方案。

诚挚的祝福

简

Dear Blair,

You are always concerned with the health and growth of students. Thank you for your issuing of the practical problems. I have thought about some solutions to improve the circumstance in the dining hall.

Actually, rules are often with little success for the students now. They have their own judgment. So I plan to organize the students to take part in the events named "career day" to experience the roles of cook and farmers. I believe they will realize what life is about and value the foods.

If you have any good suggestion, don't hesitate to tell me.

Best regards,

Jane

亲爱的布莱尔：

　　你总是很关心学生的健康和成长。非常感谢你提出这些实际的问题，我已经想出了一些改善食堂环境的方案。

　　实际上，制定规章制度对于现在的学生来说是收效甚微的，他们有自己的主见了，所以我计划组织学生参加名为"职位体验日"的活动去体验厨师和农民的生活。我相信他们会感悟到生活的真谛并且爱惜食物的。

　　如果你有好的建议，敬请提出来。

诚挚的问候
简

范本二 | 抱怨环境太吵

Dear Manager,

　　I am a customer who often live in your hotel, and now I have many complaints to say about your service. Yesterday, I felt tired when I came back from work and would like to have a good sleep at 8:00 pm. I was just falling asleep when there was a big noise from the lobby! It was the harsh sound of electric saw sweeping on the wall that made me so freaked. Then I called receptionist to stop the annoying noise, but got two earplugs! Do you think it is the good solution to solve such a serious problem?

　　I am angry and hope you can give me a satisfying solution.

Jenny

尊敬的经理：

　　我是你们酒店的老顾客，如今关于你们的服务我有许多批评意见。昨天晚上八点我下班回到酒店觉得特别累想要好好睡一觉，我刚睡着就听到走廊上有噪音！是电锯在墙上划过的声音，令我感到非常焦躁。然后我打电话给前台希望他们能停止噪音，但是前台却送来两只耳塞！你认为这样严重的问题是两个耳塞就能解决的吗？

　　我非常生气，希望你们能给我一个令人满意的解决方案。

詹尼

Dear Jenny,

　　I am so sorry after reading your letter of complaints and would like to explain to you. We employed some staff to reconstruct some parts of our hotel recently, so yesterday they were repairing the wall lamps in the evening. I feel so sorry for the annoying noise and the attitude of our receptionist.

From now on, we prepare to change the repairing time to afternoon so that it would not interrupt you. If you have any requirements, please contact us without hesitation.

Best regards,
Tony

尊敬的詹尼：

读完您的抱怨信我感到非常抱歉并向您解释一下情况：近期我们雇用了一些工作人员对酒店的部分进行修整，所以昨晚他们正在修理壁灯。我对产生的噪音和前台的服务态度向您道歉。

从今天开始，我们准备将修理时间改为下午，这样就不会打扰到您睡觉了。如果您还有什么需要，敬请提出来。

诚挚的问候
托尼

Dear Jenny,

I should apologize to you for the unpleasant incidents yesterday. It was our negligence of duty to make customer feel angry. The noise was made by the staff who was repairing the wall lamp yesterday. Now, the wall lamp has been fixed, so there will be no noise in the future. But I should apologize that we did not tell you in advance and interfere your sleep. And I must say sorry again for the "earplugs", I will let them apologize to you later.

Best wishes,
Tony

亲爱的詹尼：

我为昨天发生的不愉快的事件对您说句抱歉，令顾客感到生气是我们的失职。这个噪声是因为昨晚工作人员在修理壁灯，现在壁灯已经完全修理好了，所以不会再有噪声了。但是我们没有事先通知您从而打扰了您休息，我对此感到抱歉。另外关于"耳塞"一事我再次道歉，我一会儿会让前台专程去给您道歉。

诚挚的祝福
托尼

范本三 | 抱怨火车晚点

Dear Manager,

I travelled to Shanghai by No. 1012 train yesterday from the local train station. The time on the ticket was 2:00 pm, but the train didn't come until 5:10 pm! I had a very important meeting in Shanghai, but I missed my chance to make a deal because I was late! And I knew the train was always delayed that made many people complain again and again. Shouldn't you work out any solutions to avoid late arrival of the train?

Best regards,

Jenny

尊敬的经理：

昨天我从本地火车站出发坐1012次列车去上海，火车票上的时间是下午两点，但是火车到五点十分才来！我在上海有一个非常重要的会议，但是因为我迟到了所以丢了一单生意！并且我知道这趟列车经常晚点，惹得人们不停抱怨。难道你们就不能想出解决火车晚点的办法吗？

诚挚的祝福

詹妮

Dear Jenny,

I must apologize for causing your losses because of our negligence. The No.1012 train is always delayed because it is always overloaded. The time for terminal stop is not enough for passengers to get on or off the train which also leads to the confusing situation.

Now we will reorder the time for terminal stop and add two more trains to Shanghai and hope that can bring more convenience to passengers.

Yours sincerely,

Joy

亲爱的詹妮：

因为我们的失职让您产生了损失，我必须向您说抱歉。1012次列车经常晚点是因为车上总是超员，停站时间过短，旅客上下时间不够，所以导致了如今混乱的局面。

我们将会重新安排停站时间并且增加另外两班去上海的车次，希望能给旅客带来方便。

谨启
乔伊

Dear Jenny,

I feel so sorry to you after reading your letter. The delayed train always cause passengers' complaints and inconvenience. But there are many factors for the delay, including weather, road conditions and passenger flow volume. There is no controllable factor to improve the current situation.

In the future, we will increase the trains and spread the passenger flow, hoping to make sure all the trains arrive on time.

Do you have any good suggestions?

Yours sincerely,
Joy

亲爱的詹妮：

读完你的来信我感到非常抱歉。火车晚点总是引起乘客抱怨和不便，但是火车晚点有许多方面的因素，包括天气，路况和客流量，没有可控因素能改善目前的状况。

未来我们会增加线路并分流旅客，希望所有的车次能准时到站。

你有好的建议吗？

谨启
乔伊

范本四｜抱怨产品质量

Dear Sir,

I am writing to you about an unhappy experience. Last month, we bought a new TV from your shop. It was a great pity that we found there was something wrong with the television. After we used it for a week, we found that the image was not much clear as before and always moved up and down. Besides, sometimes it had a noise and sounded like an old TV without any signal.

This problem has affected our normal life. My family can not bear it any more. So, can you change one for me as soon as possible? Your prompt attention is appreciated.

Yours sincerely,

Tom

尊敬的先生：

　　我写信来时为了向您反映一件我们所遇到的不愉快事情。上个月我们从你们店里买了一台新电视，遗憾的是我们发现这台电视有些问题。我们用了一周之后发现图像不如之前清晰并且上下闪动，另外，有时它会发出噪声，听起来像没有信号的旧电视。

　　这个问题已经影响到了我们的正常生活，我们全家都无法忍受了。所以，您能尽快给我们换一台吗？期待您的回复。

谨启

汤姆

Dear Tom,

　　We have received the letter in which you complained about our TV. We are so sorry for the inconvenience you have experienced. Actually, all the televisions in our shop have the quality system certificates and are purchased from formal channels. So the televisions are of high quality. It is supposed that the recent rainy days is the reason for the unusual performance of the image and sound.

　　We will arrange the staff to your house to check the causes and repair the TV for free. If it is the quality problem indeed, we will change a new one for you as soon as possible.

Yours sincerely,

Kevin

亲爱的汤姆：

　　我们已经收到您抱怨电视机的来信，给您造成的不便我们向您道歉。实际上，我们店里所有的电视都有质保书，并且进货渠道正规，所以这些电视质量都是很好的。估计最近的阴雨天导致了图像和声道异常。

　　我们将会安排工作人员去您家进行检测并免费维修。如果确实是质量问题，我们会尽快给您换一台新的。

谨启

凯文

Dear Tom,

Thank you for your letter concerning the goods you ordered last month. I should apologize to you for the small problems existing inside the TV. I really understand your requirement of changing a new one. But before changing it we should find out where the crux is, so we need you to send me back the television for checking the problems. If the television has the quality problem, we will change a new one for you.

We appreciate your interest in our product. If you have any other question, please write to me.

Sincerely,

Kevin

亲爱的汤姆：

感谢您的来信。对于电视存在的小问题，我需要向您说抱歉。我非常理解您提出要换一台的要求，但是在换之前，我们需要找出问题的症结所在，所以需要您送回电视用于检测问题。如果电视存在质量问题，我们会给您换台新的。

我们非常感谢您购买我们的产品，如果您有别的问题，可以写信给我。

谨启

凯文

范本五 | 批评抱怨信（1）

Dear Sir,

The computers we ordered from you last month should have been delivered two days ago. You should know that the delay in delivery has brought us great inconvenience because we can not send the computers to our clients on time! You should arrange the delivery as soon as possible, otherwise I will make the order from other company.

Please look into the matter as one of urgency and give a reasonable reply.

Sincerely,

Eric

尊敬的先生：

我们上个月向您订购的一批电脑本该在两天前到货。要知道你们延迟发货给我们带来了很大的不便，因为我们无法按时给客户寄出电脑！你们应该尽快安排发货，否则我将从别的公司订货。

请紧急处理此事并给出合理答复。

谨启
艾瑞克

Dear Eric,

I should make an apology to you because the production of computers has not been completed. It is estimated to be finished and packed tomorrow. I promise you that I will deliver the goods to you at the end of this week.

I am so sorry to delay your time of delivery, so I offer you a 10% discount. Please let me know if you have any further questions.

Sincerely yours,
Bill

尊敬的艾瑞克先生：

我必须向您说声抱歉，因为这批电脑的生产还未完成。预计明天完成生产并能装箱，保证在这周末前我一定会发货。

我很抱歉延误了你的发货期，所以我给您打个九折。如果还有什么问题，尽管联系我。

谨启
比尔

Dear Eric,

I am so sorry to hear your suffering but I can not be responsible for the delayed delivery. It appears that the responsibility should rest on the shipping company. The production of goods had been completed last Monday and should be delivered last Wednesday. I suggest you to deal with the shipping company or the insurers who is in charge of these goods.

If you need any help, please let me know.

Yours sincerely,
Bill

尊敬的艾瑞克：

听到您的消息我感到很遗憾，但是发货延迟并非我方责任，责任方应该是运输公司，这批电脑上周已经生产完成并且上周四就应该发货。我建议您与运输公司或者负责这批货的承保人交涉一下。

如果您还需要别的帮助，请联系我。

谨启
比尔

范本六 | 批评抱怨信（2）

Dear Sir or Madam,

It is a pity to write this letter to you to complain about the service of your shop assistant. Yesterday, I went to your shop to buy a thermos cup so that I can drink hot water during my journey. We preferred two new products but could not decide to choose which one, then asked the shop assistants for help. However, one of your assistants named Lily did not act in polite. She turned a deaf ear to our request and walked away murmuring in a sarcastic manner!

At last, other assistant came and helped us to pick a better one. I was angry with the former assistant's attitude! I wish you should look into this and take steps to improve your service!

Yours sincerely,
Amy

尊敬的先生/女士：

很遗憾写这封信抱怨您店里售货员的服务。昨天我去您的店里准备买一个保温水壶，旅游的时候用得上。我们看中了两款新品但是难以抉择买哪个，然后向售货员求助，但是其中一个名为莉莉的售货员表现得非常不礼貌，她对我的问题置之不理并说着难听的话走开了！

最后，其他售货员帮助我们选了一个更好的保温壶，但是我因为之前那个售货员的态度感到非常生气！我希望你们能正视这个严重的问题并采取措施改进你们的服务！

谨启
艾米

Dear Amy,

I have to express my unusual regret for the unhappy experience we caused to you! Our duty is providing a comfortable shopping environment and detailed shopping guide for clients. All the assistants should treat our clients with enthusiasm and patience. It is our mistake to make your shopping experience so unpleasant. I have criticized Lily who behaved impolitely yesterday.

I promise to you that this situation would not happen again! Welcome to contact us and make a purchase again!

Yours sincerely,
Demon

亲爱的艾米：

对于我们给您造成的不愉快经历我感到非常抱歉！我们的责任是给顾客提供良好的购物环境和购物指导，我们所有的售货员都应该怀着热情和耐心面对客户，给您的购物带来如此的不愉快是我们的责任，我已经批评过昨天对您不礼貌的售货员莉莉。

我向您保证这样的情况将不会再发生了！欢迎您再次来函咨询和选购！

谨启
德蒙

Dear Amy,

I have to say sorry for the impolite behavior of our assistant Lily to you. Thank you for choosing our shop. It is our fault to make you feel angry. I had a meeting on purpose to teach a lesson to our staff for how to provide high quality service this morning. I will issue some rules and a system of rewards and penalties to improve the employees' motivation . Thank you for reminding me to provide better service to our clients.

Welcome to our shop again!

Sincerely yours,
Demon

亲爱的艾米：

我必须要为莉莉不礼貌的行为向您说声抱歉。感谢您来我们店里购物，让您生气是我们的过错。我早上已经特意开会教育我们的员工如何提供高品质的服务，我将会制定一些规章和奖惩制度，从而提高员工工作积极性。感谢您提醒我要改进我们的服务。

欢迎再次光临！

谨启
德蒙

范本七 | 批评抱怨信（3）

Dear Mr. Manager,

I would like to lodge a complaint regarding the poor quality of shoes which I bought last month in your store. When I tried the shoes in your store, I felt it was comfortable and purchased them immediately. However, after I wore for one day, I found they wiped my heels seriously and made them blood a little! I don't know where the problem is. It disappointed me very much. I trust you can understand that I expect the compensation for my loss.

Your prompt attention is appreciated.

Yours faithfully,

Lucy

尊敬的经理先生：

我上个月在你们店里买了一双鞋，我想要抱怨一下这双鞋的质量。当我在店里试穿的时候，我感觉它非常舒服并立刻买下了它。但是在我穿过一天之后，我发现它非常磨脚，并且使我的脚后跟有些出血！我不知道问题出在哪，这双鞋令我非常失望。我相信您应该会理解我请求损失的赔偿。

希望您尽快解决此事。

敬上

露西

Dear Lucy,

I have to express regret for your wound and losses. As you said our shoes are very comfortable and suit for feet. The principle of the design is to make feet comfortable. You should trust the quality of our shoes. The problem of wiping heel maybe is caused by the material of the shoes PU leather which is less soft than dermis. Some people are raw easily by PU leather. I suggest you not to buy the shoes made of PU leather in the future.

I am sorry we can not change one or compensate for your losses because the reason is unknowable.

Yours faithfully,

Kelly

亲爱的露西：

我对您的伤口和损失表示抱歉。正如您所说的，我们的鞋子穿起来很舒适并且契合双脚。我们的设计原则就是确保舒适，所以您应该相信我们鞋子的质量。鞋子磨脚也许是因为这双鞋的材质是PU皮的，不如真皮柔软。有些人很容易被PU皮磨破脚，我建议您以后不要买PU皮材质的鞋了。

我很抱歉我们无法换一双或者赔偿您的损失，因为磨脚的原因还不可知。

敬上

凯利

Dear Lucy,

I have to apologize to you that our shoes rub your feet. It maybe is the design problem that the stitches of the leather are just beside the heels, so they made you feel hurt. Many other clients also complained about this problem. We will reflect this to our factory and request them to fill the design gap.

Now, we can change another shoes for you in our store which are of equal value with that ones. And I will provide you a VIP card as the compensation for your losses.

Best regards,

Kelly

亲爱的露西：

我们的鞋子磨破您的脚，我对此深感抱歉。也许是因为鞋子设计问题，皮鞋的缝线刚好在脚后跟处，所以令您感到磨脚。也有许多别的客人抱怨这个问题，我们会反馈给工厂并要求他们弥补这个设计缺陷。

我们可以给您换一双店里同等价值的鞋，另外提供一张贵宾卡作为补偿。

诚挚的祝福，

凯利

读书笔记

Lesson 20　预约预订信

如何写预约预订信

a 写信包括提出约会的请求并说明原因；建议约会时间和地点等；请对方回复。

b 回信分为接受和拒绝两种。接受一般包括：表明来信收悉并接受；重述具体时间、地点等；表示希望会晤或感谢。拒绝一般包括：表明来信收悉；说明拒绝的原因；致歉。

实用例句

1. Thank you for your letter of 7 May regarding your new product.

   5月7日有关新产品的函收悉。

2. I leave it to you to choose.

   听你的选择。

3. I look forward to seeing you again.

   期待与您再见面。

4. I am planning a trip to France next month, and I am looking forward to meeting you.

   下月我将赴法国一游，期望能与您会面。

5. Please let me know when you would like to call on us.

   请让我知道你何时愿意到访我们。

6. Could you choose a place for the meeting?

   能否选定会面地点？

7. We will keep you informed on our progress and look forward to hearing from you.

   愿进一步加强联系，并候复音。

8. If for any reason you are unable to attend, please call me so that we can make other arrangements.

   若因故不能出席，烦请致电告知，以便另行安排。

9. We would appreciate it if you advise us whether you have a mind to deal with us by returning mail.

   请贵公司复函给我们，表示是否有意愿与本公司进行交易，我们将不胜感激。

10. Please feel free to suggest a time and I will arrange mine accordingly.

敬请提出会晤时间，我将全力配合。

范本一 | 请求约见（1）

Dear Mr. Bob,

 Mr. John Green, our General Manager, will be in Paris for the whole of May and would like to come to see you. We hope to talk about the opening of a sample room on May 10 at 2：00 p.m. Please let us know if the time is convenient for you. You would suggest the time by the way.

Yours faithfully,
Jenny

尊敬的鲍勃先生：

 我们的总经理约翰·格林整个五月份都将在巴黎并且想与您见面。有关开样品房的事宜，我们想在5月10日下午2：00点拜访您讨论一下，请告知这个时间对您是否方便。如不方便，请给出具体时间。

您诚挚的
珍妮

Dear Ms. Jenny,

 Thank you for your letter informing us of Mr. Green's visit. I regret to say that we can not agree to your request for the appointment. Our manager is now in London. He will not be back until the middle of June. However, he would like to meet Mr. Green any time after his return. I am looking forward to your contact.

Yours faithfully,
Lucy

亲爱的珍妮女士：

 感谢您来信通知我们关于格林先生的拜访。很遗憾我们不能约定见面，因为我们的经理现在在伦敦，直到六月中旬才会回来。然而他很希望在他回来后的任何时间约见格林先生，期待您的联系。

您诚挚的
露西

Dear Mr. Green,

Thank you for your letter of 25 April. I would like to confirm our appointment to discuss the opening of a sample room. I have scheduled the whole day for the meeting. If for any reason you are unable to attend, please phone me so that we can make alternative arrangements. I look forward to meeting you and discussing the matter.

Yours faithfully,

Bob

尊敬的格林先生：

感谢您4月25日的来信。我很高兴能够确定商讨开样品房的约见，当天我的计划只有这个会议，如果您有任何原因不能到来，请电话联系我们以便更改安排。很期待与您见面并讨论这件事。

您诚挚的

鲍勃

范本二 | 请求约见（2）

Dear Mr. Bob,

I plan to go to Canada on business at the end of this month and would like to call on you. As you know, we hope to cooperate with your company on our new product development plan. I have sent the details about the new product to you last week. But I still want to talk about it face to face so that we can give you an in-depth knowledge of our new product. I will arrive in Canada on 25 May, and please feel free to suggest a time and I will arrange mine accordingly. Looking forward to meeting with you!

Yours faithfully,

Jack

尊敬的鲍勃先生：

我计划于这个月底去加拿大出差并且希望能够拜访您。正如您所知，我们希望能和贵公司合作我们的新产品开发计划。虽然上周我已经将新产品的详细资料发送给您，但我仍然想要面谈，这样可以让您更深入地了解我们的新产品。我将在5月25日抵达加拿大，见面时间由您决定，我尽量配合。期待与您的见面！

您诚挚的

杰克

Dear Mr. Jack,

I'm glad to hear from you. I've read the information of your new product and it meets our standards. It will be a good opportunity for us to talk in more details about the new project and at the same time have an enjoyable time together. We initially decide to meet you on 27 May in my office at 2: 00 p.m. If you can come, please let us know as soon as possible so that we can prepare related data soon. We are looking forward to your kind confirmation.

Yours faithfully,
Bob

尊敬的杰克先生:

很高兴收到您的来信。我已经阅读了有关你们新产品的资料,新产品很符合我们的要求。这将是一个让我们谈论更多细节和享受愉快时光的好机会。我们初步决定5月27日下午2点在我的办公室见您,如果您来的话,请尽快告知以便我们准备相关材料。我们期待您的好消息。

您诚挚的
鲍勃

Dear Mr. Jack,

Thank you for your letter of 15 May. I'm sorry that we can't agree to your request for an appointment. We currently have the sole agency for another company and don't have other cooperation program this year. I wish we can have an opportunity to work together next year! At last, thank you for your invitation again!

Yours faithfully,
Bob

尊敬的杰克先生:

感谢您5月15日的来信。很抱歉我们不能见面,因为我们公司已经为另外一家公司独家代理,今年也没有其他的合作计划。希望我们在明年能有机会合作! 最后,再次感谢您的邀请!

您诚挚的
鲍勃

范本三 | 请求变更约会

Dear Lucy,

I regret that I must ask you to change the date to 5 May due to an unexpected matter that requires my personal time. I hope to meet you on 5 May around 10：00 am. If the time isn't suitable, please tell me soon. Hope this will not cause you too much inconvenience. Thank you!

Best regards,

Lily

亲爱的露西：

我很抱歉因为一些私人的事情要让你把约会时间改到5月5日。我希望我们在5月5日上午10点左右见面，如果你觉得时间不合适，请尽快联系我。希望没有给你带来太多的不便，谢谢！

诚挚的祝福

莉莉

Dear Lily,

Please don't feel guilty since the time is OK to me. Let's meet on 5 May in the park near my home. In addition, don't forget to take a huge tent and the food. I think we will have a nice weekend! See you then!

Best regards,

Lucy

亲爱的莉莉：

这个时间对我来说是可以的，所以不要内疚。我们就5月5日在我家附近的公园见面吧，另外不要忘了带一个大帐篷和食材哦。我想我们一定会有一个愉快的周末！到时候见！

诚挚的祝福

露西

Dear Lily,

I can't come to meet you on 5 May because I have to attend my good friend's birthday party. It's a pity that we can't enjoy the weekend together. In that case, we may gather together next time! Wish you a nice weekend!

Best regards,

Lucy

亲爱的莉莉：

　　因为我要参加好朋友的生日派对，所以5月5日不能来见你了，很遗憾我们不能一起度过周末。既然如此，我们就下次再聚吧！祝你周末愉快！

诚挚的祝福
露西

范本四 | 预订房间

Dear Sir,

　　I would like to reserve one single room and three double rooms with bath for one night. I plan to check into your hotel around 5：00 pm on 11 April. Please tell me at your earliest convenience the room rates, availability of vacancies, and whether I need to pay the deposit in advance. Grateful if you could give me a prompt reply. Thank you!

Sincerely yours,
Jack

尊敬的先生：

　　我想要预订带浴室的一个单人间和三个双人间住一晚。我打算在4月11日下午5点左右入住酒店，请尽快告知我房价，是否有空房以及是否需要提前支付押金。麻烦尽快给我回复，谢谢！

您诚挚的
杰克

Dear Mr. Jack,

　　Welcome to WanLong International Hotel! It's my honor to be at your service. I have checked that we have vacancies on 11 April. A single room is 288 RMB per night and a double room is 368 RMB per night. In addition, you need to pay the deposit when you arrive. Please tell me your full name and your telephone number. We will keep the rooms for you till 6：30 pm. Hope you enjoy your stay at our hotel!

Sincerely yours,
General Manager

尊敬的杰克先生：

　　欢迎预订万隆国际酒店！很荣幸为您服务。我已经查过4月11日是有

161

空房的，单人间288元/晚，双人间368元/晚。另外，您需要到店支付押金。请告知您的全名及联系号码，我们将为您保留房间至晚上6：30。希望您在我们酒店过得愉快！

您诚挚的

大堂经理

Dear Mr. Jack,

It's a pity that we have no single room left on 11 April. But we have enough double rooms for you and the double room is 368 RMB each night. You can make a decision to book four double rooms or choose other hotel. I'm sorry that we may cause inconvenience to you.

Sincerely yours,

General Manager

尊敬的杰克先生：

很遗憾4月11日没有单人间可以预定了，但我们有足够的双人间，每晚368元，您可以决定预定四间双人房或者选择别家酒店。很抱歉给您带来的不便。

您诚挚的

大堂经理

范本五 | 预订机票

Dear Sir,

I'd like to make a reservation for a flight from Nanjing to Beijing on Nov. 28th. I want to know what flights you have and how long the flights take. Besides, please tell me about the differences between the first class and economy class. Waiting for your reply! Thank you very much!

Sincerely yours,

Tom

尊敬的先生：

我想要预订一张11月28日从南京到北京的机票。我想要知道有哪些航班以及航行需要的时间，另外，请告诉我头等舱和经济舱的区别。期待您的回复！非常感谢！

您诚挚的

汤姆

Dear Mr. Tom,

We have two flights from Nanjing to Beijing. One flight is at 9:00 am and the other at 4:00 pm. They both will take one and a half hours. Both flights have seats available now. The first class is more comfortable and expensive. The air fare is 2320 RMB. The economy class is 1010 RMB for one way. Please tell me which flight you'd like to take and be there an hour before the departure. Thank you for the reservation and wish you have a nice trip!

Sincerely yours,

Air China Flight Reservation

尊敬的汤姆先生:

我们有两趟从南京飞往北京的航班，一班是在早上9点起飞，另一班是下午4点，航班需要一个半小时，目前两趟班次均可预订。头等舱更舒适和昂贵，需要2320元，经济舱单程需要1010元，请告诉我您想预订哪个班次并且在出发前一个小时到达。感谢您的预订，祝您旅途愉快!

您诚挚的

中国航空公司订票处

Dear Mr. Tom,

I'm sorry that there are no seats available on Nov. 28th. If that's all right, you can choose to book a ticket on Nov. 29th. There are two flights from Nanjing to Beijing. One flight is at 9:00 am and the other at 4:00 pm. Please contact with me when you have any demand. Thank you for the reservation!

Sincerely yours,

Air China Flight Reservation

尊敬的汤姆先生:

很抱歉11月28日的机票已经预订完了。如果可以的话，您可以选择预订29号的机票。我们有两班从南京到北京的航班，一班是早上9点出发，另一班是下午4点。如果您有任何需要请与我联系，感谢您的预订!

您诚挚的

中国航空公司订票处

读书笔记

Chapter 3

缩写篇

Unit 5 各种学位名称中英文对照翻译及缩写

美国学校提供的学位有很多种，依所学领域的不同，有不同的学位。以下列出的是美国高等教育中较常见的学位：

Ph.D.（Doctor of Philosophy）：博士学位。有些领域的博士课程会有不同的学位名称，如：D.A.（Doctor of Arts）、Ed.D.（Doctor of Education）

M.B.A.（Master of Business Administration）：工商学管理硕士。

M.A.（Master of Arts）文学硕士；B.A.（Bachelor of Arts）文学学士。两者皆属于人文、艺术或社会科学的领域，如文学、教育、艺术、音乐。

M.S.（Master of Science）理科硕士；B.S.（Bachelor of Science）理科学士。两者皆属于理工、科学的领域，如数学、物理、信息等。

Associate Degree（副学士学位）： 读完两年制小区大学或职业技术学校所得到的学位。

Dual Degree（双学位）：是由两个不同学院分别授予，因此得到的是两个学位。

Joint Degree：为两个不同学院联合给予一个学位，如法律经济硕士。

major主修 minor辅修

学士

Bachelor of Arts B.A.	文学士
Bachelor of Arts in Education B.A.Ed., B.A.E.	教育学文学士
Bachelor of Arts in Computer Science B.A.C.S.	计算机文学士
Bachelor of Arts in Music B.A.Mus, B.Mus	音乐艺术学士
Bachelor of Arts in Social Work B.A.S.W.	社会工作学文学士
Bachelor of Engineering B.Eng., B.E.	工学士

续表

Bachelor of Engineering in Social Science B.Eng.Soc.	社会工程学士
Bachelor of Engineering in Management B.Eng.Mgt.	管理工程学士
Bachelor of Environmental Science/ Studies B.E.Sc., B.E.S.	环境科学学士
Bachelor of Science B.S.	理学士
Bachelor of Science in Business B.S.B., B.S.Bus.	商学理学士
Bachelor of Science in Business Administration B.S.B.A.	工商管理学理学士
Bachelor of Science in Education B.S.Ed., B.S.E.	教育学理学士
Bachelor of Science in Engineering B.S.Eng., B.S.E.	工程学理学士
Bachelor of Science in Forestry B.S.F.	森林理学士
Bachelor of Science in Medicine B.S.Med.	医学理学士
Bachelor of Science in Medical Technology B.S.M.T., B.S.Med.Tech.	医技学理学士
Bachelor of Science in Nursing B.S.N., B.S.Nurs.	护理学理学士
Bachelor of Science in Nutrition B.S.N.	营养学理学士
Bachelor of Science in Social Work B.S.S.W.	社会工作学理学士
Bachelor of Science in Technology B.S.T.	科技学理学士
Bachelor of Computer Science B.C.S.	计算机理学士
Bachelor of Computer Special Science B.C.S.S.	计算机特殊理学士
Bachelor of Architecture B. Arch.	建筑学士
Bachelor of Administration B.Admin.	管理学士
Bachelor of Business Administration B.B.A.	工商管理学士
Bachelor of Education B.Ed., B.E.	教育学士
Bachelor of Fine Arts B.F.A.	艺术学士
Bachelor of General Studies B.G.S.	通识学士

Bachelor of Liberal Studies B.L.S.	文科学士
Bachelor of Health Science B.H.S.c.	健康科学学士
Bachelor of Music B.M., B.Mus.	音乐学士
Bachelor of Music Education B.M.Ed., B.M.E.	音乐教育学士
Bachelor of Nursing B.N.	护理学士
Bachelor of Professional Studies B.P.S.	专业进修学士
Bachelor of Law B.L.	法学士
Bachelor of Commerce B.Com.	商学士
Bachelor in Social Work B.S.W.	社会工作学士
Bachelor of Technology B.T.	科技学士
Bachelor of Kinesiology B.K., B.Kin.	运动机能学学士
Bachelor of Landscape Architecture B.L.A.	景观建筑学士
Bachelor of Nursing B.N.	护理学士
Bachelor of Physical B.Ph.	体育学士
Bachelor of Resource Management B.R.M	资源管理学士
Bachelor of Theology B.Th.	神学士

硕士

Master of Arts M.A.	文学硕士
Master of Accounting M.Acc.	会计学硕士
Master of Arts in Education M.A.Ed.	教育学文学硕士
Master of Architecture M.Arch.	建筑学硕士
Master of Arts in Teaching M.A.T.	教育文学硕士
Master of Business Administration M.B.A.	工商管理学硕士
Master of Civil Engineering M.C.E.	土木工程学硕士
Master of Chemical Engineering M.Ch.E., M.C.E.	化学工程学硕士
Master of Criminal Justice M.C.J.	刑事司法学硕士

续表

Master of Divinity M.Div.	神学硕士
Master of Engineering M.E.	工程学硕士
Master of Education M.Ed.	教育学硕士
Master of Economics M.Ec.	经济学硕士
Master of Electrical Engineering M.E.E.	电气工程学硕士
Master of Fine Arts M.F.A.	艺术硕士
Master of Law M.L.	法学硕士
Master of Library Science M.L.S.	图书馆学硕士
Master of Music M.M., M.Mus.	音乐硕士
Master of Music Education M.M.E., M.M.Ed.	音乐教育学硕士
Master of Nursing M.N.	护理学硕士
Master of Public Administration M.P.A.	公共行政学硕士
Master of Psychology M.Psy.	心理学硕士
Master of Science M.S.	理学硕士
Master of Science in Criminal Justice M.S.C.J.	刑事理学硕士
Master of Science in Education M.S.E., M.S.Ed.	教育理学硕士
Master of Science in Electrical Engineering M.S.E.E.	电机工程理学硕士
Master of Science in Library Science M.S.L.S.	图书馆理学硕士
Master of Science in Medical Technology M.S.M.T.	医技理学硕士
Master of Science in Nursing M.S.N.	护理理学硕士
Master of Science in Social Work M.S.S.W.	社会工作理学硕士
Master of Social Work M.S.W.	社会工作学硕士

博士

Doctor of Arts D.A.	文学博士

续表

Doctor of Dental Science D.D.S.	牙科博士
Doctor of Science D.Sc.; Sc.D.	理学博士
Doctor of Engineering D.E.	工程博士
Doctor of Education D.Ed.	教育学博士
Doctor of Musical Arts D.M.A.	音乐艺术博士
Doctor of Osteopathy D.O.	骨科博士
Doctor of Social Science D.S.S.	社会科学博士
Doctor of Veterinary Medicine D.V.M.	兽医学博士
Doctor of Jurisprudence J.D.	法理学博士
Doctor of Judicial Science J.S.D.	司法学博士
Doctor of Business Administration D.B.A.	工商管理博士
Doctor of Accountancy D.Acc.	会计学博士

读书笔记

Unit 6 商务英语常用缩写

A

a accepted	承兑
AA Auditing Administration	（中国）审计署
AAA	最佳等级
abs. abstract	摘要
a/c, A/C account	账户、账目
a/c, A/C account current	往来账户、活期存款账户
A&C addenda and corrigenda	补遗和勘误
Acc. acceptance or accepted	承兑
Accrd.Int accrued interest	应计利息
Acct. account	账户、账目
Acct. accountant	会计师、会计员
Acct. accounting	会计、会计学
Acct.No. account number	账户编号、账号
Acct.Tit. account title	账户名称、会计科目
ACN air consignment	航空托运单
a/c no. account number	账户编号、账号
Acpt. acceptance or accepted	承兑
A/CS Pay. accounts payable	应付账款
A/CS Rec. accounts receivable	应收账款
ACT advance corporation tax	预扣公司税
ACU Asia Currency Unit	亚洲货币单位
A.C.V actual cash value	实际现金价值
a.d., a/d after date	开票后、出票后
ADRS asset depreciation range system	固定资产分组折旧法
Adv. advance	预付款
ad.val., A/V ad valorem to (according value)	从价
Agt. agent	代理人

Agt. agreement	协议、契约
AJE adjusting journal entries	调整分录
Amt. amount	金额、总数
Ann. annuity	年金
A/P account paid	已付账款
A/P account payable	应付账款
A/P accounting period	会计期间
A/P advise and pay	付款通知
A/R account receivable	应收账款
A/R at the rate of	以……比例
a/r all risks	（保险）全险
Arr. arrivals, arrived	到货、到船
A/S, a/s after sight	见票即付
A/S，acc/s account sales	承销账、承销清单、售货清单
ASAP as soon as possible	尽快
ASR acceptance summary report	验收总结报告
ass. assessment	估征、征税
assimt. assignment	转让、让与
ATC average total cost	平均总成本
ATM at the money	仅付成本钱
ATM Automatic Teller Machine	自动取款机（柜员机）
ATS automated trade system	自动交易系统
ATS automatic transfer service	自动转移服务
Attn. attention	注意
Atty. attorney	代理人
auct. auction	拍卖
Aud. auditor	审计员、审计师
Av. average	平均值
a.w. all wool	纯羊毛
A/W air waybill	空运提单
A/W actual weight	实际重量

B

BA bank acceptance	银行承兑汇票
bal. balance	余额、差额
banky. bankruptcy	破产、倒闭
Bat battery	电池
b.b. bearer bond	不记名债券
B.B., B/B bill book	出纳簿
B/B bill bought	买入票据、买入汇票
b&b bed & breakfast	住宿费和早餐费
b.c. blind copy	密送的副本
BC buyer credit	买方信贷
B/C bills for collection	托收汇票
B.C. bank clearing	银行清算
b/d brought down	转下页
Bd. bond	债券
B/D bills discounted	已贴现票据
B/D bank draft	银行汇票
b.d.i. both dates inclusive, both days inclusive	包括头尾两天
B/E bill of entry	报关单
b.e., B/E bill of exchange	汇票
BEP breakeven point	保本点、盈亏临界点
b/f brought forward	承前
BF bonded factory	保税工厂
Bfcy. Beneficiary	受益人
B/G, b/g bonded goods	保税货物
BHC Bank Holding Company	银行控股公司
BIS Bank of International Settlements	国际清算银行
bit binary digit	两位数
Bk. bank	银行
Bk. book	账册
b.l., B/L bill of lading	提货单
B/L original bill of lading original	提货单正本
bldg. building	大厦

续表

BMP bank master policy	银行统一保险
BN bank note	钞票
BO branch office	分支营业处
BOM beginning of month	月初
b.o.m. bill of materials	用料清单
BOO build-operate-own	建造—运营—拥有
BOOM build-operate-own-maintain	建造—运营—拥有—维护
BOOT build-operate-own- transfer	建造—运营—拥有—转让
b.o.p. balance of payments	收支差额
BOT balance of trade	贸易余额
BOY beginning of year	年初
b.p., B/P bills payable	应付票据
Br. branch	分支机构
BR bank rate	银行贴现率
b.r., B/R bills receivable	应收票据
Brok. broker or brokerage	经纪人或经纪人佣金
b.s., BS, B/S balance sheet	资产负债表
B/S bill of sale	卖据、出货单
B share B share	B 股
B.T.T. bank telegraphic transfer	银行电汇
BV book value	票面价值

C

c. cents	分
C cash; coupon; currency	现金、息票、通货
C centigrade	摄氏（温度）
C. A. chartered accountant; chief accountant	特许会计师、主任（主管）会计师
C. A. commercial agent	商业代理、代理商
C. A. consumers' association	消费者协会
C/A capital account	资本账户
C/A current account	往来账
C/A current assets	流动资产

续表

C. A. D cash against document	交单付款
can. cancelled	注销
cap. capital	资本
CAPM capital asset pricing model	固定资产计价模式
C. A. S. cost accounting standards	成本会计标准
c. b., C. B. cash book	现金簿
CBD cash before delivery	先付款后交货
C. C. cashier's check	银行本票
C. C. contra credit	贷方对销
c/d carried down	过次页、结转下期
CD certificate of deposit	存单
c/f carry forward	过次页、结转
CG capital gain	资本利得
CG capital goods	生产资料、资本货物
C. H. custom house	海关
C. H. clearing house	票据交换所
Chgs charges	费用
Chq. cheque	支票
C/I certificate of insurance	保险凭证
CIA certified internal auditor	注册内部审计员
c. i. f. , C. I. F. cost, insurance and freight	到岸价，货价+保险+运费
C. I. T. comprehensive income tax	综合所得税
Ck. check	支票
C. L. call loan	短期拆放
C / L current liabilities	流动负债
C. M. A. certified management accountant	注册管理会计师
CMEA, Comecon Council for Mutual Economic Assistance	经济互助委员会
CML capital market line	资本市场线性
CMO Collateralised Mortgage Obligations	担保抵押贷款债务
CMV current market value	现时市场价值
CN consignment note	铁路运单

CN credit note	贷方通知书
c/o carried over	结转后期
CO, C/O cash order	现金汇票、现金订货
CO certificate of origin	产地证明书
Co. company	公司
COBOL Common Business Oriented Language	通用商业语言
CoCom Coordinating Committee for Multilateral Export Controls	多边出口控制协调委员会
cod, COD. cash on delivery	货到付款
Col. column	账栏
Coll. collateral	担保、抵押物
Coll. collection	托收
Com.; comm. commission	佣金
cont. container	集装箱
cont., contr. contract	契约、合同
conv., cv., cvt. convertible	可转换的、可兑换的
Cor. corpus	本金
Cor. correspondent	代理行
Corp. corporation	公司
CP. commercial paper	商业票据
CPA Certified Public Accountant	注册公共会计师
CPB China Patent Bureau	中国专利局
CPI consumer price index	消费者价格指数
CPM cost per thousand	每一千个为单位的成本
CPP current purchasing power	现行购买力
Cps. coupons	息票
CPT carriage paid to	运费付至……
C/R company's risk	企业风险
Cr. credit	贷记、贷方
CR carrier's risk	承运人风险
CR current rate	当日汇率、现行汇率
CR cash receipts	现金收入
CR class rate	分级运费率
CS civil servant; civil service	公务员、文职机关

CS convertible securities	可转换证券
CS capital stock	股本
CSI customer satisfaction index	顾客满意指数
csk. cask	木桶
CT corporate treasurer	公司财务主管
CT cable transfer	电汇
ct crate	板条箱
ctge cartage	货运费、搬运费、车费
Cts. cents	分
CTT capital transfer tax	资本转移税
cu cubic	立方
CU customs unions	关税联盟
cu. cm. cubic centimeter	立方厘米
cu. in. cubic inch	立方英寸
cu. m. cubic meter	立方米
cu. yd. cubic yard	立方码
cum. pref. cumulative preference (share)	累积优先（股）
cur. curr. current	本月、当月
CV convertible security	可转换债券
CVD countervailing duties	抵销关税、反倾销税
CVP analysis Cost Volume Profit analysis	本一量一利分析
CWO cash with order	订货付款
Cy. currency	货币
CY calendar year	日历年
CY container	整装货柜
CY container yard	货柜堆场、货柜集散场

D

D degree; draft	度、汇票
D/A deposit account	存款账户
D/A document against acceptance	承兑交单

d/a days after acceptance	承兑后……日（付款）
D. A. debit advice	欠款报单
D. B. day book	日记账、流水账
DB method declining balance (depreciation) method	递减余额折旧法
D. C. F. method discounted cash flow method	现金流量贴现法
D/D documentary draft	跟单汇票
D.D.; D/D demand draft	即期汇票
D/d; d/d days after date	出票后……日(付款)
d. d. dry dock	干船坞
DDB method double declining balance (depreciation) method	双倍递减余额折旧法
D. D. D. deadline delivery date	交易最后日期
def. deficit	赤字、亏损
dem. demurrage	滞期费
Depr. depreciation	折旧
d. f; D. F.; d. frt. dead freight	空舱费
D. G. dangerous goods	危险货物
diff. difference	差额
Dis. discount	折扣、贴现
dish'd; dishd dishonored	不名誉、拒付
D. I. T. double income-tax(relief)	双重所得税（免征）
div.; divd dividend	红利、股息
D-J Dow Jones & Co.	美国道一琼斯公司
DJIA Dow Jones Industrial Average (Stock Index)	道一琼斯工业股票指数
DJTA Dow Jones Transportation Average	道一琼斯运输平均数
DJUA Dow Jones Utility Average	道一琼斯公用事业平均数
DK Don't know	不知道
DL direct loan	直接贷款
DL discretionary limit	无条件限制
DLD deadline date	最后时限
Dls. ; Dol(s); Doll(s) dollars	美元

续表

DM Deutsche Mark; D-mark; Deutschmark	德国马克
DMCs developing member countries	发展中国家
DN date number	日期号
DN; D/N debit note	借记通知单
DNR do not reduce	不减少
do.; dto. ditto	同上、同前
D/O delivery order	发货单
Doc(s) documents	凭证、单据、文件
doc. att. documents attached	附单据、附件
Doc. code document code	凭证（单据）编号
D. O. G. days of grace	宽限日数
DOR date of request	要求日
DP; D/P document against payment	交单付款
DPI disposable personal income	个人可支配收入
DPOB date and place of birth	出生时间和地点
DPP damp proofing	防潮的
D. R.; DR discount rate	贴现率、折扣率
Dr debtor	债务人
D.R. deposit receipt	存单、存款收据
dr. drawer	借方
D.S; d/s days after sight(days' sight)	见票后……日(付款)
ds.; d's days	日
dstn. destination	日的地(港)
D.T.C Deposit taking company	接受存款公司
D.T.C Deposit Trust Company	储蓄信托公司
dup.; dupl.; dupte. duplicate	副本
DVP delivery versus payment	付款交货
dy.; d/y day; delivery	日、交货
dz dozen	一打

E

E. exchange; export	交易所、输出

E. & O. E. errors and omissions excepted	如有错漏，可加更正
e.a.o.n. except as otherwise noted	除非另有说明
EAT earnings after tax	税后收益
EB ex budgetary	预算外
EBIT earnings before interest and tax	扣除利息和税金前收益
EBS Electronic Broking Service	电子经纪服务系统
EBT earning before taxation	税前盈利
EC European Community; European Commission	欧洲共同体、欧洲委员会
EC export credit	出口信贷
EC error corrected	错误更正
Ec. exempli causa	例如
Ec. ex coupon	无息票
ECA export credit agency	出口信贷机构
ECAFE Economic Commission for Asia and the Far East	亚洲及远东经济委员会
ECE Economic Commission for Europe	欧洲经济委员会
ECG Export Credit Guarantee	出口信用担保
ECI export credit insurance	出口信用保险
ECR export credit refinancing	出口信贷再融资
ECT estimated completion time	估计竣工时间
ECU European Currency Unit	欧洲货币单位
E/D export declaration	出口申报单
ED ex dividend	无红利、除息、股利除外
EDD estimated delivery date	预计交割日
EDI electronic data interchange	电子数据交换
EDOC effective date of change	有效更改日期
EDP Electronic Data Processing	电子数据自理
E. E.; e.e errors excepted	如有错误，可加更正
EERI Effective Exchange Rate Indexes of Hong Kong	港汇指数
EET East European Time	东欧时间
EF export finance	出口融资
EF Exchange Fund	外汇基金

续表

EFT electronic funds transfer	电子资金转账
EFTA European Free Trade Area (Association)	欧洲自由贸易区（协会）
EGM Extraordinary General Meeting	特别股东大会
EIB Export-Import Bank	进出口银行
EIL WB Economic Integration Loan	世界银行经济一体化贷款
EL export license	出口许可证
ELI extra low impurity	极少杂质
EMF European Monetary Fund	欧洲货币基金
EMIP equivalent mean investment period	等值平均投资期
EMP end-of month payment	月末付款
EMP European main ports	欧洲主要港口
EMS European Monetary System	欧洲货币体系
EMS express mail service	邮政特快专递
EMU European Monetary Union	欧洲货币联盟
enc enclosed	停业
encl(s). enclosure	附件
encd. enclosed	附件
End. ; end. endorsement	背书
Entd. entered	登记入
EOA effective on or about	大约在……生效
EOD every other day	每隔一日
EOE European Options Exchange	欧洲期权交易
EOM end of month	月底
EOQ economic order quantity	最底订货量
EOS end of season	季末
EOU export-oriented unit	出口型单位
EOY end of year	年终
EPD earliest possible date	最早可能日期
EPN export promissory note	出口汇票
EPOS electronic point of sale	电子销售点
EPR earnings price ratio	收益价格比率
EPR effective protection rate	有效保护率

续表

EPS earnings per share	每股收益额、每股盈利额
E. P. T excess profit tax	超额利润税
EPVI excess present value index	超现值指数
EPZ export processing zone	出口加工区
ERM exchange rate mechanism	汇率机制
ERS Export Refinance Scheme	出口再融资计划
ESOP Employee Stock Ownership Plan	职工持股计划
Est. estate	财产、遗产
EST Eastern Standard Time	美国东部标准时间
et seq. et sequents	以下
ETA estimated time of arrival	预计到达时间
ETD estimated time of departure	预计出发时间
ETDZ Economic and Technological Development Zone	经济技术开发区
ETLT equal to or less than	等于或少于
ETS estimated time of sailing	预计启航时间
EU European Union	欧盟
EUA European Units of Account	欧洲记账单位
ex.; exch exchange	汇兑、况换
excl. exclusive	另外、不在内
ex cont. from contract	从合同
ex cp. ex coupon	无息票
ex div. ex dividend	无股息
Exp. export	出口
Extd. extend	展期
EXW ex works	工厂交货价

F

f feet	英尺
F dealt in flat	无息交易的
f. following (page)	接下页
f. fairs	定期集市

续表

F. A. face amount	票面金额
F. A. fixed assets	固定资产
F. A freight agent	货运代理行
FA free alongside	启运港船边交货
FABB Fellow of the British Association of Accountants and Auditors	英国会计师和审计师协会会员
FAC facility	设施、设备
f.a.c. fast as can	尽快
FACT factor analysis chart technique	因素分析图解法
fad. free delivery (discharge, dispatch)	免费送货
F. A. F. free at factory	工厂交货
FAIA Fellow of the Association of International Accountants	国际会计协会会员
F. A. Q. fair average quality	（货品）中等平均质量
F. A. S. free alongside ship	发运地船边交货价
FASB Financial Accounting Standards Boards	财务会计标准委员会
FAT fixed asset transfer	固定资产转移
FAT factory acceptance test	工厂验收试验
FB foreign bank	外国银行
F. B. E. foreign bill of exchange	外国汇票
F. C. fixed capital	固定资本
F. C. fixed charges	固定费用
F. C. future contract	远期合同
fc. franc	法郎
FCA Fellow of the Institute of Chartered Accountants	特许会计师学会会员
FCG foreign currency guarantee	外币担保
FCL full container load	整货柜装载
FCL/LCL full container load/less (than) full container load	整装/分卸
FCR forwarder's cargo receipt	货运代理行收据
FCT forwarding agent's certificate of transport	货运代理行领货证
fd. fund	资金

续表

FDB method fixed rate on declining balance method	定率递减余额折旧法
FDI foreign direct investment	外商直接投资
FDIC Federal Deposit Insurance Corporation	联邦储蓄保险公司
FE foreign exchange	外汇
FE future exchange	远期外汇
FF French franc	法国法郎
fib free into barge	驳船上的交货价
FIBC financial institution buyer credit policy	金融机构买方信贷险
FIFO first in, first out	先进先出法
fin. stadg.(stndg.) financial standing	资信状况
fin. stat. (F/S) financial statement	财务报表
fin.yr. financial year	财政年度
FINA following items not available	以下项目不可获得
FIO free in and out	自由进出
F. I. T free of income tax	免交所得税
fl. florin	盾
FLG finance lease guarantee	金融租赁担保
flt. flat	无利息
FMV fair market value	合理市价
FO free out	包括卸货费在内的运费
fo. folio	对折、页码
FOB free on board	（启运港）船上交货、离岸价格
FOB airport FOB airport	（启运）机场交货（价）
FOBST free on board stowed and trimming	包括清理及平仓的离岸价格
F.O.C. free of charge	免费
FOCUS Financial and Operations Combined Uniform Single Report	财务经营综合报告
FOK fill or kill	要么买进或卖出，要么取消
FOR free on rail (or road)	铁路或（公路）上交货价
for'd., fwd forward; forwarded	转递
FOREX foreign exchange	外汇

续表

FOS free on steamer	蒸汽船上交货（价）
FOUO for official use only	仅用于公事
FOW, f. o. w. free on wagon	（启运站）火车上交货（价）
FOX Futures and Options Exchange	期货和期权交易所
FP floating policy	浮动政策
FP fully paid	已全付的
FRA forward rate agreement	远期利率协议
FRCD floating rate certificate of deposit	浮动利率存单
frt., frgt. forward	期货、远期合约
free case; no charge for case	免费事例
FREF fixed rate export finance	固定利率出口融资
frt. & grat. freight and gratuity	运费及酬金
Frt. fwd freight forward	运费待付
Frt. ppd freight prepaid	运费已付
FS final settlement	最后结算
FSR feasibility study report	可行性研究报告
FTW free trade wharf	码头交易
FTZ free trade zone	自由贸易区
fut. futures	期货、将来
FV face value	面值
FVA fair value accounting	合理价值法
FWD forward (exchange) contract	远期合约
F.X. foreign exchange	外汇
FX broker foreign exchange broker	外汇经纪人
fxd fixed	固定的
FXRN fixed rate note	定息票据
FY fiscal year (financial year)	财政（务）年度
fy. pd. fully paid	全部付讫
FYI for your information	供您参考

G

g gallon; grain; gram (s); gold	加仑；格令；克;金

续表

G. A. general agent	总代理商、总代理人
GA go ahead	办理、可行
GAAP general Accepted Accounting Principles	通用会计准则
GAAS Generally Accepted Auditing Standard	通用审计标准
GAC General Administration of Customs	海关总署
gal., gall gallon	加仑
gas. gasoline	汽油
GATT General Agreement on Tariffs and Trade	关税及贸易总协定
GCL government concessional loan	政府优惠贷款
GDP gross domestic product	国内生产总值
gds. goods	商品、货物
GJ general journal	普通日记账
GL general ledger	总分类账
gm. gram(s)	克
GMP graduated payment mortgage	递增付款按揭
GND gross national demand	国民总需求
GNE gross national expenditures	国民支出总额
GNP gross national product	国民生产总值
GOFO gold forward rate	黄金远期利率
GP gross profit	毛利
GPP general purchasing power	总购买能力
gr. (grs.) wt. gross weight	毛重
GR gross revenue	毛收入
GS gross sales	销售总额
GSP generalised system of preferences	普惠制
GTM good this month	本月有效
GTW good this week	本星期有效

H

HAB house air bill	航空托运单
HAWB house air waybill	航空托运单
HCA historical cost accounting	历史成本会计
hdqrs. headquarters	总部
hg. hectogram	一百公克
HIBOR Hong Kong Interbank Offered Rate	香港银行同业拆借利率
hifo highest-in, first-out	高入先出法
H. in D. C. holder in due course	正当持票人
Hi-Q high quality	高质量
HIRCS high interest rate currencies	高利率货币
hi-tech high technology	高技术
HKD Hong Kong dollar	香港元
HKI Hong Kong Index	香港指数
hl. hectoliter	百升
hldg. holding	控股
Hon'd honored	如期支付的
HSCPI Hang Seng Consumer Price Index	恒生消费价格指数
HSI Hang Seng Index	恒生指数
hwevr. however	无论如何
Hz hertz	赫兹

I

I. A. intangible assets	无形资产
I & A inventory and allocations	库存和分配
IAS International Accounting Standard	国际会计标准
IB investment banking	投资银行（业）
I. B. invoice book	发票簿
IBA International Bank Association	国际银行家协会

IBBR interbank bid rate	银行间报价利率
I. B. I invoice book inward	购货发票簿
IBNR incurred but not reported	已发生未报告
I. B. O. invoice book outward	销货发票簿
IBOR inter-bank offered rate	银行间的拆借利率
ICB international competitive bidding	国际竞标
ICIA International Credit Insurance Association	国际信用保险协会
ICJ International Court of Justice	国际法庭
ICM international capital market	国际资本市场
ICONs index currency option notes	指数货币期权票据
ICOR incremental capital-output ratio	资本一产出增量比
I. C. U. International Code Used	国际使用的电码
IDB industrial development bond	工业发展债券
IDB Inter-American Development Bank	泛美开发银行
IDB inter-dealer broker	交易商之间经纪人
IDC intangible development cost	无形开发成本
IDR international depositary receipt	国际寄存单据
IE indirect export	间接出口
I. F. insufficient fund	存款不足
IFB invitation for bids	招标邀请
I. G. imperial gallon	英制加仑
IL, I/L import licence	进口许可证
ILC irrevocable letter of credit	不可撤销信用证
IMF International Monetary Fund	国际货币基金组织
imp. import	进口，输入
Inc. incorporated	注册（有限）公司
incl. inclusive	包括在内
incldd. included	已包含在内
incldg. including	包含
inl. haul inland haulage	内陆运输费用
INLO in lieu of	代替
Ins, ins. insurance	保险

inst. instant	即期、分期付款
Instal., instal. installment	分期付款
Int., int. interest	利息
inv., Inv. invoice	发票、付款通知
in trans (I. T.) in transit.	在(运输）途中
inv.doc./attach. invoice with document attached	附提货单的发票
Inv't., invt. inventory	存货
I-O input-output	输入—输出
IOU I owe you	借据
IOV inter-office voucher	内部传票
IPN industrial promissory note	工业汇票
IPO initial public offering	首次发售股票
IQ import quota	进口配额
IR Inland Revenue	国内税收
I. R. inward remittance	汇入款项
IRA individual retirement account	个人退休金账户
IRA interest rate agreement	利率协议
IRR interest rate risk	利率风险
IRR internal rate of return	内部收益率
irred. irredeemable	不可赎回的
IRS interest rate swap	利率调期
IS International System	公制度量衡
ISIC International Standard Industrial Classification	国际标准产业分类
IT information technology	信息技术
IT international tolerance	国际允许误差
I/T income tax	所得税
ITC investment tax credit	投资税收抵免
ITO International Trade Organization	国际贸易组织
ITS intermarket trading system	跨市场交易系统
investment value	投资价值

J & K

J., Jour. journal	日记账
J. A. (J/A) joint account	联合（共管）账簿
J. D. B. journal day-book	分类日记账
J/F, j/f journal folio	日记账页数
J. V. joint venture	合资经营企业
J. V. journal voucher	分录凭单
JVC joint venture company	合资公司
K. D. knocked down	拆散
K. D. knocked down price	成交价格
kg kilogram	千克
kilom. kilometer	千米
kv kilovolt	千伏
kw kilowatt	千瓦
KWH kilowatt-hour	千瓦小时

L

L listed (securities)	（证券）上市
L., (Led.) ledger	分类账
L. lira	里拉
L. liter	公升
L. A. (L/A) letter of authority	授权书
L. A. liquid assets	流动资产
L. B. letter book	书信备查簿
LB licensed bank	许可银行
lb pound	磅
LC (L/C) letter of credit	信用证
LCL/FCL less than container load/full container load	拼装/整拆
LCL/LCL less than container load/less than container load	拼装/拼拆
L.& D. loans and discounts	放款及贴现
L&D loss and damage	损失和损坏

续表

ldg. loading	装（卸）货
L/F ledger folio	分类账页数
LG letter of guarantee	保函
Li. liability	负债
LI letter of interest (intent)	意向书
lifo (LIFO) last in, first out	后进先出法
L. I. P. (LIP) life insurance policy	人寿保险单
LIRCs low interest rate currencies	低利率货币
L/M list of materials	材料清单
LMT local mean time	当地标准时间
LRP limited recourse project	有限追索项目
LRPF limited recourse project financing	有限追索项目融资
l. s. lump sum	一次付款总额
l. s. t. local standard time	当地标准时间
LT long term	长期
Ltd. limited	有限（公司）

M

m million	百万
M matured bond	到期的债券
M mega-	百万
M milli-	千分之……
m. meter, mile	米、英里
M&A merger & acquisition	兼并收购
MA my account	本人账户
Mat. maturity	到期日
Max., max maximum	最大量
M. B. memorandum book	备忘录
MBB mortgage-backed bonds	抵押支持的债券
MBO management by objectives	目标管理
M/C marginal credit	信贷限额
m/c metallic currency	金属货币

续表

MCA mutual currency account	共同货币账户
MCP mixed credit program	混合信贷计划
M/d months after deposit	出票后……月
M. D. maturity date	到期日
M. D. (M/D) memorandum of deposit	存款(放)单
M. D. malicious damage	恶意损坏
mdse. merchandise	商品
MEI marginal efficiency of investment	投资的边际效率
mem. memorandum	备忘录
MERM multilateral exchange rate model	多边汇率模型
M. F. mutual funds	共同基金
MF mezzanine financing	过渡融资
mfg. manufacturing	制造的
MFN most favoured nations	最惠国
mfrs. manufacturers	制造商
mg milligram	毫克
M/I marine insurance	海险
micro one millionth part	百万分之一
min minimum	最低值、最小量
MIP monthly investment plan	月度投资计划
Mk mark	马克
mks. marks	商标
mkt. market	市场
MLR minimum lending rate	最低贷款利率
MLTG medium-and-long-term guarantee	中长期担保
M. M. money market	货币市场
mm millimeter	毫米
MMDA money market deposit account	货币市场存款账户
MMI major market index	主要市场指数
MNC multinational corporation	跨（多）国公司
MNE multinational enterprise	跨国公司
MO (M. O.) money order	汇票
mo. month	月

续表

MOS management operating system	经营管理制度
Mos. months	月
MP market price	市价
M/P months after payment	付款后……月
MPC marginal propensity to consume	边际消费倾向
Mrge.(mtg.) mortgage	抵押
MRJ materials requisition journal	领料日记账
MRO maintenance, repair and operation	维护、修理及操作
MRP manufacturer's recommended price	厂商推荐价格
MRP material requirement planning	原料需求计划
MRP monthly report of progress	进度月报
MRR maintenance, repair and replace	维护、修理和替换
M/s months of sight	见票后……月
msg message	留言
MT medium term	中期
M/T mail transfer	信汇
mthly monthly	每月
MTI medium-term insurance	中期保险
MTN medium-term note	中期票据
MTU metric unit	米制单位

N

n. net	净值
N. A. net assets	净资产
n. a. not available	暂缺
N. A. non-acceptance	不承兑
NA not applicable	不可行
N. B. nota bene	注意
NC no charge	免费
N/C net capital	净资本
n. d. no date	无日期

N. D. net debt	净债务
n. d. non-delivery	未能到达
ND next day delivery	第二天交割
NDA net domestic asset	国内资产净值
N.E. net earnings	净收益
n. e. no effects	无效
n. e. not enough	不足
negb. negotiable	可转让的、可流通的
Neg. Inst., N. I. negotiable instruments	流通票据
nego. negotiate	谈判
N. E. S. not elsewhere specified	未另作说明
net. p. net proceeds	净收入
N/F no fund	无存款
NFD no fixed date	无固定日期
NFS not for sale	非卖品
N. G. net gain	纯收益
NH not held	不追索委托
N. I. net income	净收益
N. I. net interest	净利息
NIAT net income after tax	税后净收益
NIFO next in, first out	次进先出法
nil nothing	无
NIM net interest margin	净息差
NIT negative income tax	负所得税
N. L. net loss	净损失
NL no load	无佣金
n. m. nautical mile	海里
NM no marks	无标记
N. N. no name	无签名
NNP net national product	国民生产净值
NO. (no.) number	编号、号数
no a/c no account	无此账户
NOP net open position	净开头寸

续表

NOW a/c negotiable order of withdrawal	可转让存单账户
N/P net profit	净利
NP no protest	免作拒付证书
N. P. notes payable	应付票据
NPC nominal protection coefficient	名义保护系数
NPL non-performing loan	不良贷款
NPV method net present value method	净现值法
N. Q. A. net quick assets	速动资产净额
NQB no qualified bidders	无合格投标人
NR no rated	（信用）未分等级
N/R no responsibility	无责任
N. R. notes receivable	应收票据
N. S. F. (NSF) no sufficient fund	存款不足
NSF check no sufficient fund check	存款不足支票
nt. wt. net weight	净重
NTA net tangible assets	有形资产净值
NTBs non-tariffs barriers	非关税壁垒
ntl no time lost	立即
NTS not to scale	不按比例
NU name unknown	无名
N. W. net worth	净值
NWC net working capital	净流动资本
NX not exceeding	不超过
N. Y. net yield	净收益
NZ$ New Zealand dollar	新西兰元

O

o order	订单
o. (O.) offer	发盘、报价
OA open account	赊账、往来账
o/a on account of	记入……账户
o. a. overall	全面的、综合的

OAAS operational accounting and analysis system	经营会计分析制
OB other budgetary	其他预算
O. B. ordinary business	普通业务
O. B. (O/B) order book	订货簿
OB/OS index overbought/oversold index	超买超卖指数
OBV on-balance volume	持平数量法
o. c. over charge	收费过多
OC open cover	预约保险
o/d, o. d.,(O. D.) overdrawn	透支
OD overdraft	透支
O/d on demand	见票即付
O. E. (o. e.) omission excepted	遗漏除外
O. F. ocean freight	海运费
OFC open for cover	预约保险
O. G. ordinary goods	中等品
O. G. L. Open General License	不限额进口许可证
OI original issue	原始发行
OII overseas investment insurance	海外投资保险
ok. all correct	全部正确
o. m. s. output per manshift	每人每班产量
O. P. old price	原价格
O. P. open policy	不定额保险单
opp opposite	对方
opt. optional	可选择的
ord. ordinary	普通的
OS out of stock	无现货
O/s outstanding	未清偿、未收回的
O. T. overtime	加班
OTC over-the -counter market	市场外交易市场
OVA overhead variance analysis	间接费用差异分析
OW offer wanted	寻购启示
OWE optimum working efficiency	最佳工作效率

续表

oz ounce(s)	盎司
ozws. otherwise	否则

P

p penny; pence; per	便士；便士；每
P paid this year	该年（红利）已付
p. pint	品托（1/8加仑）
P.A. particular average; power of attorney	单独海损；委托书
P.A. personal account; private account	个人账户、私人账户
p.a., per ann. per annum	每年
P&A professional and administrative	职业的和管理的
P&I clause protection and indemnity clause	保障与赔偿条款
P&L profit and loss	盈亏，损益
P/A payment of arrival	货到付款
P/C price catalog; price current	价格目录；现行价格
P/E price/earning	市盈率
P/H pier-to-house	从码头到仓库
P/N promissory note	期票，本票
P/P posted price	(股票等)的牌价
PAC put and call	卖出和买入期权
pat. patent	专利
PAYE pay as you earn	所得税预扣法
PAYE pay as you enter	进入时支付
PBT profit before taxation	税前利润
pc piece; prices	片，块；价格
pcl. parcel	包裹
pd paid	已付
per pro. per procurationem	（拉丁）由……代理
PF project finance	项目融资
PFD preferred stock	优先股

续表

pk peck	配克（1/4蒲式耳）
PMO postal money order	邮政汇票
P.O.C. port of call	寄航港，停靠地
P.O.D. place of delivery	交货地点
P.O.D. port of destination; port of discharge	目的港；卸货港
P.O.R. payable on receipt	货到付款
P.P. payback period	（投资的）回收期
P.P.I. policy proof of interest	凭保证单证明的保险利益
POE port of entry	报关港口
POP advertising point-of-purchase advertising	购物点广告
POR pay on return	收益
PR payment received	付款收讫
PS postscript	又及
PV par value; present value	面值；现值

Q

q. quarto	四开，四开本
Q. quantity	数量
QB qualified buyers	合格的购买者
QC quality control	质量控制
QI quarterly index	季度指数
qr. quarter	四分之一，一刻钟
QT questioned trade	有问题交易
QTIB Qualified Terminal Interest Property Trust	附带可终止权益的财产信托
quad. quadruplicate	一式四份中的一份
quotn. quotation	报价
q.v. quod vide (which see)	参阅
q.y. query	查核

R

R option not traded	没有进行交易的期权
R. response; registered; return	答复；已注册；收益
r. rate; rupee; ruble	比率；卢比；卢布
RAD research and development	研究和开发
RAM diverse annuity mortgage	逆向年金抵押
RAN revenue anticipation note	收入预期债券
R&A rail and air	铁路及航空运输
R&D research and development	研究与开发
R&T rail and truck	铁路及卡车运输
R&W rail and water	铁路及水路运输
R/A refer to acceptor	洽询（汇票）承兑人
R/D refer to drawer	（银行）洽询出票人
RB regular budget	经常预算
RCA relative comparative advantage	相对比较优势
RCMM registered competitive market maker	注册的竞争市场自营商
rcvd. received	已收到
r.d. running days=consecutive days	连续日
RDTC registered deposit taking company	注册接受存款公司
Re. subject	主题
re. with reference to	关于
RECEIVED B/L received for shipment bill of lading	待装运提单
REER real effective exchange rate	实效汇率
ref. referee; reference; refer(red)	仲裁者；裁判；参考；呈递
REO real estate owned	拥有的不动产
REP import replacement	进口替代
REP Office representative office	代办处，代表处
REPO, repu, RP Repurchase Agreement	再回购协议
req. requisition	要货单，请求
REVOLVER revolving letter of credit	循环信用证
REWR read and write	读和写

RIEs recognized investment exchanges	认可的投资交易（所）
RI roll	卷
RLB restricted license bank	有限制牌照银行
RM remittance	汇款
rm room	房间
RMB RENMINBI	人民币，中国货币
RMS Royal Mail Steamer	皇家邮轮
RMSD Royal Mail Special Delivery	皇家邮政专递
RMT Rail and Maritime Transport Union	铁路海运联盟
ROA return on asset	资产回报率
ROC return on capital	资本收益率
ROE return on equity	股本回报率
ROI return on investment	投资收益
ROP registered option principal	记名期权本金
ro-ro roll-on/roll-off vessel	滚装船
ROS return on sales	销售收益率
RPB Recognized Professional Body	认可职业（投资）机构
RPI retail price index	零售物价指数
RPM resale price maintenance	零售价格维持措施（计划）
rpt. repeat	重复
RRP Reverse Repurchase Agreement	逆回购协议
RSL rate sensitive liability	利率敏感性债务
RSVP please reply	请回复
RT Royalty Trust	特权信托
RTM registered trade mark	注册商标
Rto ratio	比率
RTO round trip operation	往返作业
RTS rate of technical substitution	技术替代率
RTW right to work	工作权利
RUF revolving underwriting facility	循环式包销安排
RYL referring to your letter	参照你方来信
RYT referring to your telex	参照你方电传

S

S no option offered	无期权出售
S split or stock divided	拆股或股息
S signed	已签字
s second; shilling	秒；第二；先令
SA semi-annual payment	半年支付
SA South Africa	南非
SAA special arbitrage account	特别套作账户
SAB special assessment bond	特别估价债券
sae stamped addressed envelope	已贴邮票、写好地址的信封
SAFE State Administration of Foreign Exchange	国家外汇管理局
SAIC State Administration for Industry and Commerce	（中国）国家工商行政管理局
SAP Statement of Auditing Procedure	《审计程序汇编》
SAR Special Administrative Region	特别行政区
SAS Statement of Auditing Standard	《审计准则汇编》
SASE self-addressed stamped envelope	邮资已付有回邮地址的信封
SAT (China) State Administration of Taxation	（中国）国家税务局
SATCOM satellite communication	卫星通信
SB short bill	短期国库券；短期汇票
SB sales book; saving bond; savings bank	售货簿；储蓄债券；储蓄银行
SBC Swiss Bank Corp.	瑞士银行公司
SBIC Small Business Investment Corporation	小企业投资公司
SBIP small business insurance policy	小型企业保险单
SBLI Savings Bank Life Insurance	储蓄银行人寿保险
SBN Standard Book Number	标准图书号
SC sales contract	销售合同
sc scilicet namely	即
SC supplier credit	卖方信贷
SCF supplier credit finance	卖方信贷融资

Sch schilling	（奥地利）先令
SCIRR special CIRR	特别商业参考利率
SCL security characteristic line	证券特征线
SCORE special claim on residual equity	对剩余财产净值的特别要求权
SD standard deduction	标准扣除额
SDB special district bond	特区债券
SDBL sight draft, bill of lading attached	即期汇票，附带提货单
SDH synchronous digital hierarchy	同步数字系统
SDR straight discount rate	直线贴现率
SDRs special drawing rights	特别提款权
SE shareholders' equity	股东产权
SE Stock Exchange	股票交易所
SEA Single European Act	《单一欧洲法案》
SEAF Stock Exchange Automatic Exchange Facility	股票交易所自动交易措施
SEATO Southeast Asia Treaty Organization	东南亚公约组织
sec second(ary); secretary	第二，次级；秘书
sect. section	部分
Sen senator	参议院
Sept. September	九月
SET selective employment tax	单一税率工资税
SEC special economic zone	经济特区
SF sinking fund	偿债基金
Sfr Swiss Frank	瑞士法郎
SFS Summary Financial Statements	财务报表概要
sgd. signed	已签署
SHEX Sundays and holidays excepted	星期日和假日除外
SHINC Sundays and holidays included	星期日和假日包括在内
shpd. shipped	已装运
shpg. shipping	正装运

续表

shpt. shipment	装运，船货
SI Statutory Instrument; System of Units	有效立法；国际量制
SIC Standard Industrial Classification	标准产业分类
SIP structured insurance products	结构保险产品
SITC Standard International Trade Classification	国际贸易标准分类
sk sack	袋，包
SKD separate knock-known	部分散件
SLC standby LC	备用信用证
SMA special miscellaneous account	特别杂项账户
SMEs small and medium-sized enterprises	中小型企业
SMI Swiss Market Index	瑞士市场指数
SML security market line	证券市场线
SMTP supplemental medium term policy	辅助中期保险
SN stock number	股票编号
SOE state-owned enterprises	国有企业
SOF State Ownership Fund	国家所有权基金
sola sola bill, sola draft, sola of exchange	（拉丁）单张汇票
sov. sovereign	金镑=20先令
SOYD sum of the year's digits method	年数加总折旧法
spec. specification	规格；尺寸
SPF spare parts financing	零部件融资
SPQR small profits, quick returns	薄利多销
SPS special purpose securities	特设证券
Sq. square	平方；结清
SRM standard repair manua	标准维修手册
SRP Salary Reduction Plan I	薪水折扣计划
SRT Spousal Remainder Trust	配偶幸存者信托
ss semis, one half	一半
SS social security	社会福利
ST short term	短期

续表

ST special treatment (listed stock)	特别措施（对有问题的上市股票）
St. Dft. sight draft	即期汇票
STB special tax bond	特别税债务
STIP short-term insurance policy	短期保险单
sub subscription; substitute	订阅，签署，捐助；代替
Sun Sunday	星期日
sund. sundries	杂货，杂费
sup. supply	供应，供货

T

t time; temperature	时间；温度
T. ton; tare	吨；包装重量，皮重
TA telegraphic address=cable address	电报挂号
TA total asset	全部资产，资产
TA trade acceptance	商业承兑票据
TA transfer agent	过户转账代理人
TAB tax anticipation bill	（美国）预期抵税国库券
TACPF tied aid capital projects fund	援助联系的资本项目基金
TAF tied aid financing	援助性融资
TAL traffic and accident loss	（保险）交通和意外事故损失
TAT truck-air-truck	陆空联运
TB treasury bond, treasury bill	国库券，国库债券
T.B. trial balance	试算表
t.b.a. to be advised; to be agreed; to be announced; to be arranged	待通知；待同意；待宣布；待安排
t.b.d. to be determined	待（决定）
TBD policy to be declared policy	预保单，待报保险单
TBL through bill of lading	联运提单，直达提单
TBV trust borrower vehicle	信托借款人工具（公司）
TBW Thompson Bankwatch, a rating agent	托马逊银行评估公司
TC tariff circular	关税通报
TC telegraph collation	校对电报

续表

T.C. traveler's check	旅行支票
TCI trade credit insurance	贸易信用保险
TCIC technical credit insurance consultants	技术信用保险顾问
TCM traditional Chinese medicine	中国传统医学，中医
TD time deposit	定期存款
TD Treasury Department	（美国）财政部
TDA Trade Development Authority	贸易发展当局
TDC technical development corporation	技术开发公司
TDC Trade Development Council	（香港）贸易发展局
TDR Treasury Deposit Receipt	国库券存据
Tech technical	技术的
Tel. telephone number	电话号码
telecom telecommunications	通信
temp temperature; temporary (secretary)	温度；临时（秘书）
TESSA Tax Exempt Special Savings Account	免税特别储蓄账户
TEU twenty-foot-equipment unit	（货柜、集装箱）20英尺当量单位
TF trade finance	贸易融资
t.f. till forbid	直到取消为止
tgm. telegram	电报
three T's type, terms, technique	交易三要素，即交易类型，交易条件，销售技术
thro., thru. through	经由，通过
Thu. Thursday	星期四
TIP to insure promptness	确保迅速
TIR carnet Transports Internationaux Routier	（法国）国际公路运输证
tks. thanks	致谢，感谢
tkt ticket	票
TL time loan; total loss; trade-last	定期贷款；总损失；最后交易
TLO, T.L.O. total loss only=free from/ of all average	全损赔偿险

TLX telex=teleprinter/teletypewriter exchange	电传
TM trademark	商标
TM telegram with multiple addresses	分送电报
TMA Terminal Market Association	最终市场协会
TMO telegraph money order	电汇单
TN treasury note	国库券
TNC transnational/multinational company	跨国公司
TOD time of delivery	发货时间
Tonn. tonnage	吨位（数）
TOP Trade Opportunities Program	（美国）贸易机会计划
T.O.P. turn over, please	请翻转
TPM total productive maintenance	总生产维修（护）制
TPND theft, pilerage, and non-delivery	偷窃及不能送达险
tpo telephoto	电传照片，传真
TQ tariff quota	关税配额
T.Q., t.q. tale quale	（拉丁）按现状，现状条件
TQC total quality control	全面质量控制
TR telegram restante; trust receipt	留交电报；信托收据
T.R. tons registered	（船舶）注册吨位
Tr. transfer	过户，转让
traditio symbolia	（拉丁）象征性交费
Tranche CD certificate of deposit	份额存单
trans translated	译本
treas treasurer	会计，出纳，库管，司库
Trip. triplicate	一式三份中的一份
Triple A 3A	3A级，最佳债券评级
TRS terminal receiving system	港外待运仓收货制度
TRT Trademark Registration Treaty	商标注册条约
TSP Total Suspended Particle	总空中悬浮物（污染指标）
TST test	检查，检测
TT Testamentary Trust	遗嘱信托
TT, T/T telegraphic transfer	电汇

续表

T.T.B. telegraphic transfer bought	买入电汇
T.T.S. telegraphic transfer sold	卖出电汇
TTY teletypewriter	电报打字员
TU Trade Union	工会，职工协会
Tue, Tues Tuesday	星期二
TV terminal value; television	最终价值；电视
TW transit warehouse	转口仓库
TWI training within industry	业内训练
txt. text	课文，电文，正文
Ty. territory	领土，（推销员的）推销区域
T&E Card travel and entertainment card	旅行和娱乐信用卡
T&H temperature and humidity	温度和湿度
T&M time and material	时间和材料
T/C time charter	定期租船，计时租船
t/km ton kilometer	吨/千米

U

U union; upper; fashionable; polite	联盟；上等；时髦；礼貌
U, U. unit; United	单位；联合的；联合（公司）
U.A. unit of account	记账单位，计价单位
U.K./Cont. United Kingdom or Continent	英国或欧洲大陆（港口）
U.K.f.o. United Kingdom for orders	英国沿岸的指定港口
U.L.C.C. ultra large crude carrier	超大型油轮
U/A underwriting account	保险账户
u/c. undercharge	不足的价钱，少讨的价钱
U/M unscheduled maintenance	计划外维护
U/W, UW underwriters	保险公司，承销人
UAE the Union of Arab Emirates	（阿拉伯联合酋长国）阿联酋
Uberrimae fidei of the utmost good faith	最诚信的
UBR uniform business rate	统一商业税率

续表

UBS Union Bank of Switzerland	瑞士联合银行
UCP Uniform Customs and Practice (for Documentary Credit)	（跟单信用证）统一惯例与事物
UGT, ugt urgent	（电报用语）急电，加急
UHF ultra high frequency	超高频
UIT Unit Investment Trust	单位投资信托
UITF Urgent Issue Task Force	（财务报表）紧急补救解释处
Ull. ullage	缺量，损耗
ult. ultimo	（拉丁）（商业函电）上月的
Ultra vires beyond the powers of	超过……的权限（有限公司）
UN United Nations	联合国
undelvd. undelivered	未装运的
Univ university	大学
unkwn. unknown.	未知的
unrevd. unreceived	未收到的
UNSYM unsymmetrical	不对称的
UOS unless otherwise specified	除非有特别说明
UPC Uniform Practice Code	《统一作法法典》
UPR unearned premiums reserve	未获得保险金储备
ur. your	你的
US United States; Unlisted securities	美国；未上市证券
USD United States dollar	美元
USG United States gallon	美国加仑
USIT Unit Share Investment Trust	单位股投资信托
USM Unlisted Securities Market	为挂牌（上市）证券市场
UT universal time	世界标准时间，格林尼治时间
UUE use until exhausted	用完为止
UV under voltage; ultraviolet	电压不足；紫外线

V

v refer to	参见
v., vs versus	（拉丁）对
V Roman 5; victory; volt	（罗马数字）5；胜利；（电压）伏

续表

V.A. value analysis	价值分析
VAB vertical assembly building	垂直装配建筑物
vac vacation	假期
vac. vacant	（职位）空缺，（旅馆、公寓）空房间
VAT value added tax	增值税
VC Vice Chairman; Vice Chancellor; Vice Consul	副主席；副首相；副总理；副领事
VD volume deleted	勾销的数量
VE value engineering	价值工程
Veep Vice president	副总裁
VER voluntary export restraint	自愿出口限制
Ves. vessel	船舶
via. through, by way of	经由，通过
vid vide (see)	（拉丁）参看，请看
VIP Very Important Person	贵宾
vis major	（拉丁）不可抗力
viz. videlicet, namely	（拉丁）即，也就是
VL value line investment survey	价值线投资概览法
V-mail video-mail	声像电子邮讯系统
VOD video on demand	交互电视技术系统
vol. volume	量，额，本，卷，容积
voy. voyage	航海，航程
VQA vendor quality assurance	售主质量保证
VQC vendor quality certification	售主质量确认
VQD vendor quality defect	售主质量缺陷
VRM variable rate mortgage	可变利率抵押
VS/N vendor serial number	售主系列号
VSI vendor shipping instruction	售主船运说明
VSO Voluntary Service Overseas	海外义务服务
VSQ very special quality	特级质量
VSSP vendor standard settlement program	售主标准程序结算
VTC Voting Trust Certificate	股东投票权信托证书
VTP vendor test program	售主检测计划

续表

VTR video tape record	录像带录像

W

weight ton; winter mark for load line; won	重量吨；（船舶）冬季装载线标记；（韩国）元
W., w. warehouse; watt; weight; width; week	仓库；瓦特；钟量；宽；星期
W.A. with average	水渍险，保单独海损险
W.A.C.C.C. Worldwide Air Cargo Commodity Classfication	全球空运商品分类
W.A.I.O.P. W.A. irrespective of percentage	单独海损不计免赔率，单独海损全赔
WAEC West African Economic Community	西非经济共同体
WAG wagon	卡车
WAN Wide Area Networks	泛区网络
WASH Washington; washer	华盛顿；洗衣机
WB, W.B. waybill	运送单
WB World Bank	世界银行
W.B. water ballast	（以）水压载，水压舱
W.B.S. without benefit to/of salvage	不享有获救财产的利益
w.c., W.C. without charge; water closet	免费；洗手间
WCG working capital guarantee	流动资金担保
WCO World Customs Organization	世界海关组织
WD when distributed	（股票）发售时交割
wd. warrented	（品质）保证的
wdth. width	广度，宽度
Wed Wednesday	星期三
WEF World Economic Forum	世界经济论坛
W.E.T. Western European Time	西欧时间，即格林尼治时间
wf. wharf	码头
WFOE wholly foreign owned enterprises	外资独资企业

续表

W.G., w.g. weight guaranteed	保证重量
WH watt-hour	每小时瓦特
WHO World Health Organization	世界卫生组织
whs, whse. warehouse	仓库
whsle wholesale	批发
WI when issued	（股票）发行时交割
WIP work in progress=goods in progress	在制品
wk week; work	星期；工作
Wky. weekly	每星期的，周刊
wmk watermark	水印
Wmk. water mark	水位标记
WOC without compensation	无补偿
WP weather permitting; word processing	天气允许；文字处理
W.P. without prejudice	不损害（当事人）权利
W.P.A. with particular average=with average	水渍险
W.P.M. words per minute	（电传）每分钟字数
W.P.P. waterproof paper packing	防潮纸包装
W.R. war risk	战争险
W.R.=W.W. warehouse receipt=warehouse warrant	仓单，仓库收据
Wrap worldwide receivables assurance protection	全球应收账款担保措施
WT warrant	（股票）认证股
WT watertight	（包、盒）不漏水的，防水的
WT, W/T wireless telegraphy, wireless telephone	无线电报；无线电话
wt., wgt. weight	重量
WTO World Trade Organization	世界贸易组织
W/Tax withholding tax	预扣税
WW warehouse warrant; with warrants	仓库保证；附认股权
w/w wall-to-wall	覆盖全部地面的（地毯）
W/W warehouse-to-warehouse	仓库至仓库

续表

W/W clause warehouse-to-warehouse clause	仓库至仓库条款
www worldwide web	万维网，全球计算机网

X

X ten dollars	（美国俚语）10美元
X ex-interest	无利息
X Roman 10; a kiss; an unknown number, thing, name, etc.	（罗马数字）10；一吻；未知数（物、名等等）
X. ten; X; out of	十；X；在外
x.a. ex all	无所有权益
x.b., xb; XB ex bonus; extra budgetary	不附（本期）红利；预算外的
X.C., X. cp. ex coupon	无息债券
x.d. ex distribution	不包括（下期股息或红利）分配
X-Dis ex-distribution	无分销
X. d., X. div. ex dividend	未付红利
X-efficiency	X效率
XI, X. in, X. int. ex interest	利息除外
XL extra large; extra long	特大；特长
Xm., X'mas Christmas	圣诞节
X-mark a signature	"X"符号签字（盲人或受伤的人可以画"X"作为签字）
Xn Christian	基督的
XN, XW ex-warrant	除证
X.n., X. new ex new	无权要求新股
X.P. expres paye=extra message paid	额外通信费付讫；已令函奉上
XR, x.r. ex -right	无优惠权认购新股，除权
XS extra small	特小
Xtry. extraordinary	非常的，临时的
× × × international emergency signal	国际紧急信号

Y & Z

Y ex-dividend and sales in full	不计红利，全数出售
Y Yen	元（日本货币单位）
Y Yuan	元（中国货币单位）
y yard; year; yen	码（三英尺）；年；日元
Y.A.R. York-Antwerp Rules	约克-安特卫普规则（海险）
YB, yrbk yearbook	年报，年鉴
y'day, yest. yesterday	昨天
YLD yield	收益
YOB year of birth	出生年份
YOD year of death	死亡年份
YOM year of marriage	结婚年份
yo-yo stock	"悠悠"股票（波动大、不稳定的高价特种股票）
yr year; your	年；你的
YTB yield to broker	经济商收益
YTC yield to (first) call	至通知赎回时收益
YTM yield to maturity	全期收益，到期收益
z zero; zone	零；区
ZBA zero bracket amount	零基数预算法
ZBB zero-based budgeting	零基数预算法，免税金额，免征点
ZDD zero defect program	无缺陷计划
ZIP code	邮政编码
Z. P. G. zero population growth	人口零增长
ZR zero coupon issue	零息发行
zswk this week	本周
ZT zone time	区时

Unit 7 常用外贸英语缩写一览表

B组

BAF	燃油附加费 Bunker Adjustment Factor
B/L	海运提单 Bill of Lading
B/R	买价 Buying Rate

C组（主要运费已付）

CFR	(Cost and Freight)成本加运费价
C&F	成本加运费Cost And Freight
C&F	成本加海运费 Cost And Freight
CIF	成本、保险加海运费 Cost，Insurance and Freight
CIF	成本运费加保险，俗称"到岸价" Cost, Insurance and Freight
CPT	运费付至目的地 Carriage Paid To
CIP	运费、保险费付至目的地 Carriage and Insurance Paid To
CY/CY	整柜交货（起点/终点）
C.Y.	货柜场 Container Yard
CY	码头Container Yard
CFS	场 Cargo Freight Station
C/D	报关单Customs Declaration
C.C	运费到付 Collect
CNTR NO.	柜号 Container Number
C.O	一般原产地证 Certificate of Origin
CTN/ CTNS	纸箱 Carton/Cartons
C.S.C	货柜服务费 Container Service Charge
C/(CNEE)	收货人 Consignee
C/O	产地证 Certificate of Origin
CAF	货币汇率附加费 Currency Adjustment Factor
CFS	散货仓库 Container Freight Station

续表

CFS/CFS	散装交货（起点/终点）
CHB	报关行 Customs House Broker
COMM	商品 Commodity
CTNR	柜子 Container

D组（到达）

DAF	边境交货 Delivered At Frontier
DES	目的港船上交货 Delivered Ex Ship
DEQ	目的港码头交货 Delivered Ex Quay
DDU	未完税交货 Delivered Duty Unpaid
DDP	完税后交货 Delivered Duty Paid
DDC	目的港码头费Destination Delivery Charge
DL/DLS	美元Dollar/Dollars
D/P	付款交单 Document Against Payment
DOC	文件、单据Document
DOC	文件费 Document Charge
Doc#	文件号码 Document Number
D/A	承兑交单 Document Against Acceptance
DOZ/DZ	一打 Dozen
D/O	到港通知 Delivery Order

E组（发货）

EXW	工厂交货（……指定地点）
Ex	工厂交货 Work/ExFactory
ETA	到港日 Estimated Time Of Arrival
ETD	开船日 Estimated Time Of Delivery
ETC	截关日 Estimated Time Of Closing
EBS、EBA	部分航线燃油附加费的表示方式，EBS一般是澳洲航线使用
EBA	一般是非洲航线、中南美航线使用
EXP	出口 export
EA	每个，各 each
EPS	设备位置附加费Equipment Position Surcharges

F组（主要运费未付）

FCA	货交承运人 Free Carrier
FAS	船边交货（……指定装运港）Free Alongside Ship
FOB	船上交货 Free On Board
FOB	离岸价 FREE ON BOARD
FCL	整箱货 FULL CONTAINER CARGO LOAD
FCL	整柜 Full Container Load
LCL	拼箱货 LESS THAN ONECONTAINER CARGO LOAD
FAF	燃油价调整附加费（日本航线专用）
FAF	燃料附加费 Fuel Adjustment Factor
FAC	传真 facsimile
Form A	产地证（贸易公司）
F/F	货运代理 Freight Forwarder
FAK	各种货品 Freight All Kind
FAS	装运港船边交货 Free Alongside Ship
Feeder Vessel/ Lighter	驳船航次
FMC	联邦海事委员会 Federal Maritime Commission
FIO	是FREE IN AND OUT的意思，指船公司不付装船和卸船费用
FIOST	条款，指船公司不负责装，卸，平舱，理舱
FI	是FREE IN的意思，指船公司不付装
FO	是FREE OUT的意思，同理指船公司不付卸

G组

GRI	综合费率上涨附加费，一般是南美航线、美国航线使用
GRI	全面涨价 General Rate Increase
G.W.	毛重 Gross Weight
G.S.P.	普惠制 Generalized System of Preferences

H组

HB/L	货代提单 HOUSE BILL OF LADING
HBL	子提单 House B/L

续表

H/C	代理费 Handling Charge

I组

IFA	临时燃油附加费，某些航线临时使用
INT	国际的 International
INV	发票 Invoice
IMP	进口 Import
I/S	内销售 Inside Sales
IA	各别调价 Independent Action
IAC	多式联运附加费 Administrative Charge

J组

JP	代表"日元"

L组

FCL	整箱货 FULL CONTAINER CARGO LOAD
LCL	拼箱货 LESS THAN ONECONTAINER CARGO LOAD
LCL	拼柜 Less Than Container Load
L/C	信用证 Letter of Credit
Land Bridge	陆桥

M组

MB/L	主提单 Master Bill Of Loading
MIN	最小的，最低限度 minimum
M/V	商船 merchant vessel
MT或M/T	公吨 metric ton
M/T	尺码吨（即货物收费以尺码计费）Measurement Ton
MAX	最大的、最大限度的 maximum
M 或MED	中等，中级的 medium
MLB	小陆桥，自一港到另一港口 Minni Land Bridge

续表

Mother Vessel	主线船
MTD	多式联运单据 Multimodal Transport Document

N组

NOVCC	无船承运人 NON VESSEL OPRERATING COMMON CARRIER
NVOCC	无船承运人 Non Vessel Operating Common Carrier
N.W.	净重 Net Weight
N/F	通知人 Notify

O组

O/F	海运费 Ocean Freight
ORC	（广东地区原产地收货费）：ORIGINAL RECEIVING CHARGE
OB/L	（海运提单）：OCEAN BILL OF LADING
OBL	海运提单 Ocean (or original)B/L
ORC	本地出口附加费，和SPS类似，一般在华南地区使用
ORC	本地收货费用（广东省收取）Origen Recevie Charges
OCP	货主自行安排运到内陆点 Overland Continental Point
OP	操作 Operation

P组

POD	目的港 Port Of Destination
POL	装运港 Port Of Loading
PSS	旺季附加费 Peak Season Sucharges
REF	参考、查价 Reference
RMB	人民币 Renminbi
PR或PRC	价格 Price
P/P	运费预付 Freight Prepaid
P.P	预付 Prepaid
PCS	港口拥挤附加费 Port Congestion Surcharge
PTF	巴拿马运河附加费，美国航线、中南美航线使用
PKG	一包，一捆，一扎，一件等 package

PCE/PCS	(只、个、支等 piece/pieces)
P/L	装箱单、明细表 Packing List
PCT	百分比 Percent
PUR	购买、购货 Purchase

S组

S/O	订舱单SHIPPING ORDER
S/O	装货指示书 Shipping Order
SEAL NO.	铅封号
S/C	销售确认书 Sales Contract
S/C	售货合同 Sales Contract
SC	服务合同 Service Contract
STL.	式样、款式、类型 Style
SPS	上海港口附加费（船挂上港九区、十区）
S.S	船运 Steamship
S/M	装船标记 Shipping Marks
S/(Shpr)	发货人 Shipper
S/R	卖价 Selling Rate
S/S	Spread Sheet Spread Sheet
SSL	船公司 Steam Ship Line
SDR	特别提款权 Special Drawing Rights

T组

THC	码头操作费（香港收取) Terminal Handling Charges
T/T	电汇 Telegram Transit
T/T	航程 Transit Time
T.O.C	码头操作费 Terminal Operations Option
T.R.C	码头收柜费 Terminal Receiving Charge
T/S	转船，转运 Trans-Ship
TVC/ TVR	定期定量合同 Time Volume Contract/ Rate
TTL	总共 Total
T 或 L T X 或 TX(telex)	电传

V组

VESSEL/ VOYAGE	（船名/航次）
VOCC	船公司 Vessel Operating Common Carrier

W组

W	具有 with
WT	重量 weight
W/T	重量吨(即货物收费以重量计费) Weight Ton
w/o	没有 without
W/M	即以重量吨或者尺码吨中从高收费 Weight or Measurement Ton

Y组

YAS	日元升值附加费（日本航线专用）
YAS	码头附加费 Yard Surcharges
HS-Code	海关编码即HS编码，为编码协调制度的简称The Harmonization Code

价格条件

价格术语 trade term (price term)

运费 freight

单价 price

码头费 wharfage

总值 total value

卸货费 landing charges

金额 amount

关税 customs duty

净价 net price

印花税 stamp duty

含佣价 price including commission

港口税 portdues

回佣 return commission

装运港 portof shipment

折扣 discount,allowance

卸货港 port of discharge

批发价 wholesale price

目的港portof destination

零售价 retail price

进口许口证 inportlicence

现货价格 spot price

出口许口证 exportlicence

期货价格 forward price

现行价格（时价）current price prevailingprice

国际市场价格 world (International) Marketprice

离岸价（船上交货价）FOB-free on board

成本加运费价（离岸加运费价）C&F- cost and freight

交货条件

到岸价（成本加运费、保险费价）CIF- cost,insurance and freighte

交货 delivery

轮船 steamship(缩写S.S)

装运、装船 shipment

租船 charter (the chartered shep)

交货时间 time of delivery

定程租船 voyage charter

装运期限 time of shipment

定期租船 time charter

托运人（一般指出口商）shipper,consignor

收货人 consignee

班轮 regular shipping liner

驳船 lighter

舱位 shipping space

油轮 tanker

报关 clearance of goods

陆运收据 cargo receipt

提货 to take delivery of goods

空运提单 airway bill

正本提单 original BL

选择港（任意港）optional port

选港费 optional charges

选港费（由买方负担）optional charges to be borne by the Buyers 或 optional charges for Buyers account

一月份装船 shipment during January 或 January shipment

一月底装船 shipment not later than Jan.31st.或shipment on or before Jan.31st.

一/二月份装船 shipment during Jan./Feb.或 Jan./Feb. shipment

在……（时间）分两批装船 shipment during....in two lots

在……（时间）平均分两批装船 shipment during....in two equal lots

分三个月装运 in three monthly shipments

分三个月，每月平均装运 in three equal monthly shipments

立即装运 immediate shipments

即期装运 prompt shipments

收到信用证后30天内装运 shipments within 30 days after receipt of L/C

允许分批装船 partial shipment not allowed partial shipment not permitted partial shipment not unacceptable

交易磋商、合同签订

订单 indent

订货；订购 book; booking

电复 cable reply

实盘 firm offer

递盘 bid; bidding

递实盘 bid firm

还盘 counter offer

发盘（发价）offer

发实盘 offer firm

询盘（询价）inquiry; enquiry

交易磋商、合同签订

指示性价格 price indication

速复 reply immediately

参考价 reference price

习惯做法 usual practice

交易磋商 business negotiation

不受约束 without engagement

业务洽谈 business discussion

限复 subject to reply

限复到 subject to reply reaching here

有效期限 time of validity

有效至：valid till

购货合同 purchase contract

销售合同 sales contract

购货确认书 purchase confirmation

销售确认书 sales confirmation

一般交易条件 general terms and conditions

以未售出为准 subject to prior sale

需经卖方确认 subject to sellers confirmation

需经我方最后确认 subject to our final confirmation

贸易方式

拍卖 auction

寄售 consignment

招标 invitation of tender

投标 submission of tender

一般代理人 agent

总代理人 general agent

代理协议 agency agreement

累计佣金 accumulative commission

补偿贸易 compensation trade

抵偿贸易 compensating/compensatory trade

往返贸易 counter trade

来料加工 processing on giving materials

来料装配 assembling on provided parts

独家经营/专营权 exclusive right

独家经营/包销/代理协议 exclusivity agreement

独家代理 sole agency; sole agent; exclusive agency; exclusive agent

品质条件

品质 quality

原样 original sample

规格 specifications

复样 duplicate sample

说明 description

对等样品 countersample

标准 standard type

参考样品 reference sample

商品目录 catalogue

封样 sealed sample

宣传小册 pamphlet

公差 tolerance

货号 article No.

花色（搭配）assortment

样品 sample

增减 plus or minus

代表性样品 representative sample

大路货（良好平均品质）fair average quality

商检仲裁

索赔 claim

争议 disputes

罚金条款 penalty

仲裁 arbitration

不可抗力 force Majeure

仲裁庭 arbitral tribunal

产地证明书 certificate of origin

品质检验证书 inspection certificate of quanlity

重量检验证书 inspection certificate of weight (quantity)

商品检验局 commodity inspection bureau (C.I.B)

品质、重量检验证书 inspection certificate

数量条件

个数 number

净重 net weight

容积 capacity

毛作净 gross for net

体积 volume

皮重 tare

毛重 gross weight

溢短装条款 more or less clause

外汇

外汇 foreign exchange

法定贬值 devaluation

外币 foreign currency

法定升值 revaluation

汇率 rate of exchange

浮动汇率 floating rate

国际收支 balance of payments

硬通货 hard currency

直接标价 direct quotation

软通货 soft currency

间接标价 indirect quotation

金平价 gold standard

买入汇率 buying rate

通货膨胀 inflation

卖出汇率 selling rate

固定汇率 fixed rate

金本位制度 gold standard

黄金输送点 gold points

铸币平价 mint par

纸币制度 paper money system

国际货币基金 international monetary fund

黄金外汇储备 gold and foreign exchange reserve

汇率波动的官定上下限 official upper and lower limits of fluctuation

读书笔记

Unit 8　考试缩写

LEC	法律英语证书
BEC	剑桥商务英语证书考试
CPA	注册会计师
CAAC	英国特许注册会计师考试
CIA	注册内部审计师考试
IELTS	雅思
GRE	硕士考试
BEC	商务英语
TSE	英语口语考试
GMAT	国外工商管理硕士MBA入学考试
PETS	全国英语等级考试
CET	大学四六级英语考试

读书笔记

Unit 9   常用的应用系统缩写

ERP	企业资源计划 Enterprise Resource Planning
CRM	客户关系管理 Customer Relationship Management
EAI	企业应用集成 Enterprise Application Integration
DRP	分销资源计划 Distribution Resource Planning
CAPP	计算机辅助工艺过程设计 Computer Aided Process Planning
PDM	产品数据管理 Product Data Management
OA	办公自动化系统 Office Automation
MES	生产管理系统/制造执行管理系统 Manufacturing Execution System
BPM	业务流程管理 Business Process Management
SCM	供应链管理 Supply Chain Management
DMS	文档管理系统 Document Management System
EIP	企业信息门户 Portal Enterprise Information
PM	项目管理 Project Management
KM	知识管理 Knowledge Management
BI	商业智能 Business Intelligence
ASP	应用服务提供（IT外包）Application Service Provider
PLM	生命周期管理 Product Lifecycle Management
PDM	产品数据管理 Product Data Management
CC	协同管理
EAM	企业资产管理 Enterprise Asset Management
HRM	人力资源管理 Human Resource Management

Unit 10　职务缩写

CEO

CEO（Chief Executive Officer），即首席执行官，是美国人在20世纪60年代进行公司治理结构改革创新时的产物，它的出现在某种意义上代表着将原来董事会手中的一些决策权过渡到经营层手中。

在我国，CEO这个概念最早出现在一些网络企业中。在那里，CEO往往是自封的，也很少有人去研究这一称谓对企业到底意味着什么。但是，当"CEO"在中国叫得越来越响的时候，我们应该认识到，高层人员称谓的改变不是一件小事，设立CEO职位不应仅仅是对时尚的追赶。

CFO

CFO（Chief Financial Officer）意指公司首席财政官或财务总监，是现代公司中最重要、最有价值的顶尖管理职位之一，是掌握着企业的神经系统（财务信息）和循环系统（现金资源）的灵魂人物。

做一名成功的CFO需要具备丰富的金融理论知识和实务经验。公司理财与金融市场交互、项目估价、风险管理、产品研发、战略规划、企业核心竞争力的识别与建立以及洞悉信息技术及电子商务对企业的冲击等都是CFO职责范围内的事。

在一个大型公司运作中，CFO是一个穿插在金融市场操作和公司内部财务管理之间的角色。担当CFO的人才大多是拥有多年在金融市场驰骋经验的人。在美国，优秀的CFO常常在华尔街做过成功的基金经理人。

COO

首席营运官COO Chief Operation Officer 的职责主要是负责公司的日常营运，辅助CEO的工作。一般来讲，COO负责公司职能管理组织体系的建设，并代表CEO处理企业的日常职能事务。如果公司未设有总裁职务，则COO还要承担整体业务管理的职能，主管企业营销与综合业务拓展，负责建立公司整个的销售策略与政策，组织生产经营，协助CEO制订公司的业务发展计划，并对公司的经营绩效进行考核。

这里还有：

首席品牌官	【CBO】Chief Brand Officer
首席文化官	【CCO】Chief Cultural Officer
开发总监	【CDO】Chief Development Officer
首席执行官	【CEO】Chief Executive Officer
首席财务官	【CFO】Chief Finance Officer
人事总监	【CHO】Chief Human Resource Officer
首席信息官	【CIO】Chief Information Officer
首席知识官	【CKO】Chief Knowledge Officer
首席市场官	【CMO】Chief Marketing Officer
首席谈判官	【CNO】Chief Negotiation Officer
首席营运官	【COO】Chief Operation Officer
公关总监	【CPO】Chief Public Relation Officer
质量总监	【CQO】Chief Quality Officer
销售总监	【CSO】Chief Sales Officer
首席技术官	【CTO】Chief Technology Officer
评估总监	【CVO】Chief Valuation Officer

CAO：Answerer 首席答辩人，专门负责解答媒体、债权人和用户等有关网站倒闭问题的询问。

CBO：Business Plan 首席商业计划官，是首席财务官的助理之一，专门针对不同的投资人制订相应的BP。

CCO：Cost Control 首席成本控制官，凡超过100元以上的支出必须由CCO批准。

CDO：Domain Name 首席域名官，负责公司域名注册、网站清盘时域名的拍卖、域名法律纠纷等相关问题。

CEO：Exchange 首席交换官，一般由国际CEO自由联盟随时更换，是一个常设的短期职能岗位，类似足球教练。

CFO：Financial 首席财务官，公司最重要的领导人，决定公司命运的主要人物。

CGO：Guideline 首席方针制订官，规划公司的宏伟蓝图，一般是5年以后的目标。

CHO：Harmony 首席协调官，调解投资者和经营者之间的冲突，并确保公司内部矛盾不要泄露。

CIO：Inspector 首席检查官，检查公司内部工作状况，监督员工工作态度。

CJO：Judge 首席执法官，解决内部劳资纠纷，包括员工对降薪、辞退补偿等所引起的问题。

CKO：Keep Connecting，网络连接专员，最繁忙的岗位之一，当中国电信的网络连接中断时及时向员工通报。

CLO：Lawyer 首席律师，负责公司被控侵权时的应诉以及各种合同文本的审核。

CMO：Media 首席媒体官，保持和媒体之间的友好关系，为公司随时发布新闻做准备。

CNO：News 首席新闻官，向媒体披露公司网站被黑、裁员、被收购等重大新闻。

COO：Observer 首席观察员，每天在各大网站BBS灌水，有时也被称为"大虾"，工作向CWO直接汇报。

CPO：Privacy 首席隐私官，负责公司内部员工E-mail、ICQ、OICQ等通信内容的监控。

CQO：Quantity Making，数量指标编造专家，负责注册用户数量、页面浏览、营业收入等指标的编造。

CRO：Reduce the staff trimmer 首席裁员官，负责所有与裁员有关的事务，直接向股东大会负责，包括董事长在内都不得干预其工作。

CSO：Strategy 首席战略官，由已经退位的公司主要创建人担任，在政府机关一般称为调研员或顾问。

CTO：Testing 首席测试官，是公司唯一负责网站建设的专家，由于技术开发不成熟，需要一直测试下去。

CUO：Union 首席联盟官，以战略联盟的名义，专门寻找有收购自己意向的网站。

CVO：VC Reception 风险投资商接待专员，首席财务官的另一重要助理。

CWO：Writer 首席网络写手，负责将小事扩大化，通过炒作达到扩大网站知名度的目的，其下属为COO。

CXO：Xingxiang（因为中国特有，所以只能用汉语拼音表示）网站形象代言人，一般由学历不高且没有任何网络知识的年轻人担任。

CYO：Yearly 公司元老，这是一个荣誉称号，授予在同一网站工作满一年的员工（这个职位通常空缺）。

CZO：Zero 最后离开公司的一个人，负责关好门窗，将公司大门钥匙交给物业管理处，可以由CAO兼任。